THE BANANA PEEL DIARIES

By:

Sheryl St. George

Paperwrights

© 2024 - Sheryl St. George

All rights reserved. No part of this publication may be reproduced, stored in a retrieval system, or transmitted in any form or by any means – electronic, mechanical, photocopy, recording, or any other – except for brief quotations in printed reviews, without the prior permission of the author.

ISBN: 9798330231386

Table of Contents

The House on the Hill

When I was two years old, I fell on my head. I didn't slip on a banana peel but none the less, my fall was pretty spectacular. I know you're thinking that it's not uncommon for two-year-old children to fall and hit their head, but I guess from an early age, I felt compelled to stand out in a crowd. We lived in a rural area in southern Indiana at the time and had planned to spend the afternoon visiting some friends of my parents. These people lived in a house nestled deep within the woods, and the quiet country roads that led from our house to theirs were canopied with tree branches that stretched across the road. As we drove through the countryside, flashes of sunlight danced on my face as we passed underneath the umbrella of foliage. The intensity of the sudden breaks in shadow caused me to close my eyes, enjoying the warmth of the sunlight and its strobe-like effect. After traveling down many winding roads, away from any semblance of civilization, we turned onto their dirt driveway and arrived at their doorstep.

Any time my parents called upon them, they played cards for hours. On this particular afternoon, a competitive card game consumed the adults. When most people play cards, they do it casually, for enjoyment. However, when my family engages in a game of cards, we embrace it as a life and death situation. In his never-ending competitive spirit, my father furiously and relentlessly tried to prove to the other players that he was the best card player in the world. Mom had ventured out for a break to use the outdoor facilities, since back then only the rich people had indoor plumbing. The outhouse sat a ways away from the house, by design, for reasons that I am sure you can figure out. Therefore, taking a break wasn't just a two-minute ordeal. As it happened, while Mom was otherwise occupied, one of my parents' friends had the dreadful assignment of watching me when I decided to dive head first off the back of their balcony, which just happened to be twenty feet off the ground. You would think that such a feat would call for an audience bigger than one person, but he happened to be the only witness to this daring performance of precision and agility. Since their house sat in a forested area and plenty of bushes and soft greenery surrounded their home, many options existed for me to have a soft landing; however, I decidedly picked a rock instead. Thankfully, I survived the incident with a slight concussion and about a dozen stitches. I think it aged Mom and Dad a few extra years and gave them a fresh, new understanding of my hardheadedness. As for the sole witness, I can safely say it took him a while to recover. I also believe this event was the first indication that things would not necessarily go as planned throughout my life, especially when I strayed very far from home.

I spent the first few years of my life living in the small, southern Indiana town of New Albany. My parents struggled to make ends meet, as a young couple with two small children. We lived in a house that stood on the side of a hill. Fulfilling the American dream of home ownership, my parents bought the house in the late 1950s for around $5,000. It was nothing special, but they proudly owned it, and I have many fond memories of that time. I don't remember how many square feet the house encompassed, but to me, as a small child, the house seemed huge. It had a coal-burning furnace and a trap door laid on the porch leading down into the basement where Dad stored the coal. Sometimes during the night people would break into the basement and steal our coal, or so Dad thought.. Dad charged down the basement steps in his boxer shorts any time he heard an unfamiliar sound in the night. He never stopped to grab his gun or even a baseball bat, and I think he still doesn't know what he would have done if he had ever encountered anyone. He just knew that he paid hard-earned money for that coal and he would protect his investment as best he could. He never did catch anyone in the act, and sometimes

I think he just dreamt that someone stole the coal, since things don't ever seem to last as long as you think they will. I think his imagination helped him justify the dwindling coal pile.

The house had a screened-in porch on the front of it, perfect for visiting, and at that time, Dad enjoyed making homemade beer. When he brewed up a batch, his best friend Eddy would come over and they would sample the wares. They sat on that porch for hours and talked about cars and sports, drinking home brew. As young men, barely out of their teens and newly out on their own, what else would they do? After all, Dad had barely reached the ripe old age of twenty when we lived in the house on the hill, so he was not much more than a child himself.

One Easter, the Easter Bunny brought my sister Tara and me each an Easter duckling. The active ducks begged for water, so Mom filled a ten-gallon metal washtub where they could swim around and she put it out on our porch. The ducklings glided gracefully over the water, as their little, webbed feet paddled synchronously with each other. Tara and I loved watching the ripples on the surface of the water undulate gently away from the ducks' ever-moving feet. One afternoon, as Dad and Eddy relaxed on the porch, their bonding ritual, they watched the ducks paddle around. For reasons yet unknown to mankind, they decided to see if the ducks liked beer (well, maybe the reasons aren't entirely mysterious: Dad and Eddy had certainly already been enjoying their own several brews). The ducks must have been male—as everyone knows the beer gene resides in the "y" chromosome—because they loved it. Dad put some beer in a dish for them and they repeatedly dipped their bills into the bowl and then pointed their heads skyward as they swallowed the beer.

When Dad placed them back in the tub of water, they had clearly developed a bit of a balance problem. As they paddled around, they gradually tipped over, as if in slow motion, until the water submerged their heads and their feet paddled up in the air, still in time with each other. Delighted, Dad and Eddy cackled and slapped their thighs. Then they sat the ducklings back upright again, monitoring the spectacle as the same series of events repeated time after time. Tears of laughter streamed down their cheeks for a time, but as with young children, men drinking beer don't have a very long attention span and thus, they eventually lost interest and wandered off. Unfortunately, without attentive assistance, the poor drunk ducklings drowned. Conversely of the many similarities that exist between small children and men in their early twenties, one distinct difference is that the men had no fear of the matriarchal influence in the house. That was, until later that day. Mom didn't have to say a word. Her pursed lips and hands-on-the-hips posture was the silent lecture no living human could misunderstand. Tara and I were too young to suffer much from the impact of our ducks' early demise, perhaps due to our own short attention spans. However, I quickly realized that Mom had made them both acutely remorseful of their mindless deed after watching the body language at the dinner table that evening. Let's face it: someone had to play the role of the adult in the family.

****

Mealtime was an enjoyable part of the day for us when Tara and I grew up. We have always been close, and we commonly shared just about everything. This practice started in early childhood at the dinner table. Tara never cared for vegetables as a child, and Mom wanted to ensure that Tara and I received nutrition from all four food groups. Tara thought the four food groups consisted of potatoes, bread, peanut butter, and jelly, and she didn't have any trouble eating from those categories. But when it came to the most dreaded food group of all, the *green* food group, Tara couldn't persuade herself to consume the items on her plate.

Mom's rules stated that you couldn't leave the table until your plate had nothing left on it. As a child, Mom's voice ruled the house. I never imagined breaking Mom's rules, either out respect for her or fear of the consequences, I don't know. Regardless, I thought Mom's rules were sacred, chiseled in stone and secured in an impenetrable tomb somewhere in the hills of Indiana. In contrast, Tara didn't share my unwavering conviction and fear.

So Tara couldn't get up from the table until she ate everything on her plate, and I wouldn't leave as long as available food for consumption remained on the table. Tara and I had ravenous appetites, but she was pickier about what she put in her mouth. Me, I would eat anything that wasn't moving. It seemed that I could never get enough to eat. But Tara always struggled with the thought of having to eat green beans, spinach, asparagus, or anything else that grew in a garden. Eventually, the evening meal became a battle ground, a contest of wills between Tara and Mom. Sooner or later, though, Mom would leave the room, pretending to have a pressing agenda, and in her absence, Tara fed me her green stuff. I wasn't finicky at all, and I always had the satisfaction of knowing that even though I was the littlest one in the house, I always got my share of the grub. Later in life we found out that Mom knew all along that Tara fed me her vegetables, but just didn't want Tara to know that she knew. When Mom returned to the kitchen, we both displayed a wide-eyed *bird-that-just-ate-the-canary* expression on our faces. It's funny what you think that you secretly accomplished while you grew up, only to find out that your parents knew all the time. We thought we had run a successful, covert operation throughout our childhood, when, in reality, Mom knew the entire time—and had the satisfaction of knowing that at least one of us ingested enough vitamin A in our diet.

We lived on the outskirts of New Albany during this time and a wooded area resided behind our house. In order to get to the area, Tara and I had to climb a huge embankment, which was probably only about two or three feet high. But to us it appeared gargantuan. Twenty feet or so into the woods, a clearing unfolded, where an old table and chairs sat, abandoned by its previous owner. An old, square, rickety cabinet also stood in the clearing, so we pretended that it was our kitchen. We visited the area daily and played for hours. Tara's favorite game consisted of making mud pies. She proudly convinced me that the mud pies were fit for consumption. I can still remember the taste of cool mud and the feel of grit in my mouth. Tara told me those mud pies would taste like chocolate, and since I always yearned for something to eat and since those pies roughly resembled the same color as chocolate, I believed her. I apparently possessed a vivid imagination, because I ate them in their entirety. We pretended that they were my desserts. One evening after consuming a healthy portion of Tara's concoction, I developed a bit of a problem with the ole number two. My stomach cramped incessantly and for the first time in my young life, I lost my appetite. It felt like the chocolate mud delight that I enjoyed earlier had quickly turned to freshly set cement. At the dinner table, Mom became increasingly alarmed, since I never had turned down food before. Tara insisted that our escapades remain a secret from Mom and as such, I remained silent. Convinced that I verged on the edge of a medical criticality, Mom started to put on her shoes in preparation of yet another visit to the Emergency Room. As she picked me up to carry me to the car, I blurted out the privileged information that I had vowed to take to my grave. "Tara fed me mud pies!" Instantly, Mom's lips tightened as she glared at Tara, shooting plastic butter knives at her (no sharp objects allowed). Tara ended up in the time-out chair and that ended my daily desserts (although I can't really say that I missed them). It's surprising that, even after my steady diet of mud pies, I didn't assume the role of the picky eater.

Tara and I both loved running errands with Mom. We didn't care where we went or what we did. The thought of a new adventure away from home filled us with excitement. One day when we ventured out with Mom, she decided to stop back by the house to retrieve something that she had forgotten. Tara and I stayed in the car as Mom quickly ran into the house. Since Mom planned to be gone for only a minute, she left the car running. Tara, being an inquisitive three year old, decided to investigate the lever on the steering column, and accidentally put the car into gear. Remember, our house sat up on a pretty substantial hill; therefore, Tara didn't even need to push on the gas to get the tires rolling. A concrete retaining wall that someone, in his or her ultimate wisdom had constructed luckily obstructed our path. If it wouldn't have been for the foresight of this very insightful person, I may not be sitting here today. The car accelerated fast enough that the front end cleared the wall; however, the rear didn't traverse the structure. So there we sat, trying to look innocent, as Mom came running out of the house screaming and waving her arms. I wasn't scared, because at my age I didn't understand danger. I just felt like I had been on Mr. Toad's Wild Ride and enjoyed the excitement. However, when I saw the alarm in Mom's eyes, I decided to take the "I have no idea what happened" stance. One tow truck driver and a couple hours later, and we hit the road again. One last note on that topic is that I can tell you that Tara's driving skills have only slightly improved since that day.

Tara and I used to play for hours and one of our favorite activities consisted of sliding down the hallway on rugs. The house had hardwood floors throughout, and I always thought it was swell that you could stoop down on the floor and look through the cracks between the boards to view the coal underneath the house. Since the house sat on the side of a hill, the side away from the ground stood up on stilts. I didn't think it worrisome that you could see through the cracks in the floor, nor did Tara or I think it strange that we could run a few steps and slide on a rug all the way down the hallway. After all, Mom always kept the floors nicely waxed, so they were easy to slide on. We took off running and hit the rug about mid-way through the living room, slid all the way through the bedroom, and ended up on the back porch. What we didn't know at the time was that our amazing sliding abilities were not due to our superior strength or skill, but because the house had started leaning, so we were sliding on a downhill slope. We just thought that we were blessed with exceptionally good athletic talents and pretended to be training for the Olympic luge event. After all, I already knew I was qualified for the high dive, and of course, Tara had already had her first lesson in stock car racing—or maybe I should say the demolition derby.

Obviously to anyone, Tara and I immensely enjoyed our first home; that is, until the city condemned the house and forced us to move. As you can imagine, Mom and Dad had no hope of recouping their investment in the house; so much for the American dream of home-ownership. I knew that I would miss the house on the hill, as we had racked up so many hours of fun playing in the different rooms. But the time had come to return to our roots. All of our grandparents started out as farmers, and so we moved back to the country. Mom's Uncle Ben had given her and Dad a small piece of land to do with what they wanted. So they poured a small, concrete patio, purchased a ten by fifty trailer, and had it put on the property. It was only about ten minutes out of town, so Mom and Dad continued working in New Albany while living in the country. I was three years old when we moved to the farm and full of the kind of irrepressible excitement and bursting energy that only small children seem to be fully capable of. I eagerly anticipated all the new (mis)adventures Tara and I would experience in our new home, for there were sure to be many more.

The Farm

The farm was a terrific place for a child to grow up. As anticipated, numerous adventures filled our days and equally numerous mishaps. In particular, Tara and I played for hours in an abandoned house that sat on the property. Although we had indoor plumbing by that time (I thought we had become very rich people indeed), an old outhouse lurked at the edge of our property. It turned out to be very handy the year the pipes froze and Mom and Dad couldn't afford to repair them. Even though disgusting smells emanated from its bowels, it beat squatting in the bushes. Every night before bed, after we dressed in our pajamas, Dad got the flashlight, and we made our trek to the outhouse. When we took baths, Mom fetched two buckets of water out of the well, and heated them on the stove. Times were tough, but by the following year, Mom and Dad had saved enough money to repair the plumbing and we were back in business. From that time on, the old outhouse became nothing more than a quaint conversation piece.

After the outhouse experience, the most dreaded thing about using the indoor facilities occurred when you went into the bathroom and a pile of newspapers lay on the floor. This signaled that our toilet paper supply had run out and payday hadn't yet arrived. I would just sigh, sit down on the toilet, and start crumpling pages. First we would crumple the page thoroughly and then stretch the page out, repeating this ritual many times, in an attempt to soften our makeshift toilet paper. My hands turned black by the time I finished, but at least the paper felt softer. (You'll notice as you continue reading this book, I am somewhat fixated on the subject of bathrooms, but I think after reading my story you will agree it's for good reason.)

A creek ran across the road close to our farm, and in the summertime, Tara and I strolled down to it and frolicked in the water. In the spring, swarms of tadpoles saturated the creek. We filled coke bottles with water from the creek, captured as many tadpoles as we could, and then placed them in the bottles. We continued this ritual until the coke bottles contained a black, pulsating mass of life. The little swimmers delighted us and we compared our bottles, holding them side-by-side, determining who had collected the most creatures. Then we set the tadpoles free after our attention moved on to something else. Needless to say, there was never a shortage of frogs in the area.

When we lived on the farm, Tara attended first and second grade. Not being school-aged yet, I spent my days with my Grandma Nola, who lived two miles up the road, while Mom and Dad worked. Nola's was Mom's mother and the serious one of the family. I never saw her in a pair of pants and I'm fairly certain she didn't own any. In the summer, she wore cotton dresses that she referred to as dusters. I marveled at her fortitude, as she spent her days completing her share of the farm chores while the men worked the fields. During harvest time, she sat for hours snapping green beans, filling jars and preparing them for winter storage in the cellar. She never shied away from a task or asked for assistance, although her short stature (she was only five feet tall) sometimes presented a challenge for her. Thankfully there was no shortage of step stools in the house, which came in handy for me as well.

Our Aunt Mary lived at Grandma Nola's house. Mary blessed Nola later in life. Contraceptives weren't an option, because God's will ruled the McDaniel household. So my grandparents just took their chances. I don't want to refer to Mary as an accident, because I think everything happens for a reason, but my grandparents were cautiously delighted, albeit definitely surprised, by her entrance into their lives. Being the youngest sibling by eleven years, she absorbed the attention given to her, not only by her parents, but also by her older siblings. Most people would call her spoiled, but Mary's nonchalant concern for the rules infected Tara and me, since she allowed us to do all kinds of things that the adults wouldn't approve of. We thought she was the best aunt in the world, and we had a ton of fun when Grandma Nola went to the store and left Mary in charge. One of our favorite activities consisted of removing the feather mattresses from the upstairs beds and using them as sleds to slide down the stairs. If you're not familiar with featherbeds, imagine huge beanbags filled with feathers instead of Styrofoam pellets. At Grandma Nola's house, a narrow staircase connected the second floor to the bottom floor, with walls on each side. It resembled a long, narrow chute, and we slid like maniacs down the stairs on top of the feather beds. When we reached the bottom, it felt like falling on a pile of fresh snow. Of course, if Nola ever discovered our antics, Mary would have been in a heap of trouble. Luckily, we managed to keep those escapades secret.

Tara and I always had something to do when we visited Grandma Nola's farm. In the spring, hundreds of wild daffodils grew in the fields. We collected them and brought them to the house. Aunt Mary put them in a vase and placed them on the table. We also picked milkweed, and Mary would whip us up some water with food coloring in it, and after placing both in a vase, we watched in fascination as the white flowers absorbed the color over the course of the day. We pretended we were mad scientists conducting experiments, and on the farm there was an endless supply of ingredients for our various schemes and concoctions.

Grandma Nola also had a couple of peacocks on her farm, and Tara and I searched the grounds for the best feathers to complement our flower or weed arrangements. Many times we would follow the peacocks around, waiting for them to drop a tail feather. We never got too close to them, though, because they were aggressive if you didn't keep your distance. Grandma Nola bought the peacocks because they helped keep the snake population at bay. Mom freaked out at the sight of a snake, and Grandma Nola did everything within her power to quell Mom's fears. Despite her efforts, every so often a snake crept into the front yard and Grandma Nola grabbed anything within her reach to kill it. I came to the realization of how truly robust her character was the day I watched her beat a snake to death with a dust mop. On that day as I sat next to the piano, twiddling with the ivories, Grandma Nola swept the kitchen using a dust mop. As she glided the mop across the hardwood floor, she hummed at tune, most certainly her favorite hymn from last Sunday's service. When she approached the front door, she suddenly shrieked and urgently flew outside. I heard a horrible ruckus and followed her path, anxious to see what was unfolding. She stood in the front yard, stooped over, wielding that dust mop with the expertise of an experienced swordsman. With every stroke, the snake flipped around, coiled and uncoiled, trying to escape her attack, but to no avail. After a very long five minutes, the snake laid lifeless in the front yard. Grandma Nola wiped her brow, proceeded to the kitchen, resumed her humming and finished mopping the kitchen as if she were never interrupted.

A few weeks later, while at the dinner table, she iterated to the men that there was a gopher digging up her flowers (yes, as if the farm and house chores weren't enough to keep her busy, she maintained a beautifully landscaped yard as well!). She instructed them to catch the gopher before it demolished her flower bed. Uncle Ben got a cage out of the barn, but was unsuccessful at catching the varmint after numerous attempts. Several days later, while Nola weeded her flower bed, the unluckiest gopher in the world decided to dig a tunnel right in front of her. Immediately, she submerged both of her arms in the dirt, up to her elbows, completely unconcerned about her exposed fanny sticking straight up in the air, round and full for everyone to witness. She struggled, first leaning to the right, then to the left, and in one continuous move, pulled that gopher out of the ground with her bare hands. It hissed, growled and battled to escape, but Grandma Nola's firm grip held. Calmly, she rose to her feet, walked over to the cage and tossed the critter in, securing the latch tightly. I watched in sheer awe of that dauntless spirit of hers, all wrapped up in a five-foot package. After watching that display of unfaltering persistence, coupled with observing the use to which she put a common household item, I didn't step out of line very often.

We spent a lot of time at our paternal grandparents' house as well during that stage of our lives. On Friday nights, Mom and Dad bowled with Grandpa Willard and Grandma Grace, and Tara and I usually begged to go home with our grandparents. Most of the time, Mom and Dad relented, since frequently they ended up over there on Saturday night playing cards anyway.

Grace and Willard had a large and bountiful backyard where Tara and I spent much of our time. Lush honeysuckle vines covered the back fence of the yard, and when we stood downwind of the bushes, the sweet smell of nectar filled the air. Tara and I spent many afternoons standing by that back fence, pulling the flowers off the honeysuckle bushes and sucking out the nectar. It tasted sweeter than any honey I have ever sampled, to this day.

Tara and I also enjoyed playing in our grandparents' basement, which Grace and Willard never finished. The raw-wood stairs leading down to the basement floor exposed openings to the rear and their steepness presented a challenge for Tara's and my small legs. We traversed them carefully, considering the constant warnings of the adults. The smooth, concrete floor always felt cool to the touch, no matter what the outside temperature rose or fell to. The walls were clad with cement as well, but heavily pitted with small air pockets that collapsed decades before. Tara and I pressed our faces against the wall and gazed into the holes. Up close, the indentions appeared enormous, but randomly sized, and we pretended we were astronauts, getting our first close up of the craters on the moon. Metal poles, primed with a rust-colored paint held up the unvarnished beams on the ceiling that doubled for supports for the floor above. An endless number of cardboard boxes, stacked six high, stood against one side of the basement wall, holding decades of long forgotten treasures. We loved to ride our tricycles around and around, circling the perimeter of the basement floor. At the time, Dad owned a Texaco gas station and he had given Tara and me each a red fireman's helmet that displayed the Texaco logo. The helmets contained working speakers, so when we pushed a button, we could talk into the helmets and they projected our voices exactly like a bullhorn. We drove our tricycles around in circles, bellowing, "Car 54, where are you?" We had no idea of the relevance (or more correctly irrelevance) of our chatter, but nonetheless spent hours down there on our tricycles, giggling like crazy every time one of us would shout out that infamous catchphrase.

We also had crayons, pencils, and sketching paper downstairs, and we would sometimes draw or color for hours. One day when I was about five or six, we played downstairs polishing our burgeoning artistic abilities. Grandma Grace had recently purchased four new TV pillows—oversized and cushy so people could throw them on the floor and sit on them while they watched television—and we used them as squashy tables. The vinyl-covered pillows seemed fairly durable, and we didn't think anything of using them in that manner. The only disadvantage, it seemed, of using the soft pillows as tables was that our freshly sharpened pencils made drawing difficult, because the honed lead continually penetrated the paper. We didn't think to move our paper to a firmer foundation on which to draw, logical thought not being the strong point of a five- or six-year-old mind. We just kept pushing harder with our pencils, trying to make the arrangement work. Besides, we wanted to use the pillows; they were new and exciting, the latest fad in home comfort.

I don't know whether it was Tara or me who did it first (or maybe I've just repressed the memory because I don't want to take responsibility for it), but one of our pencils accidentally pierced the vinyl covering on one of the pillows: crumbled foam shot straight up in the air as a *whooshing* sound emanated from the punctured pillow, as it released air pressure. Shocked, but devilishly intrigued, we sat there motionless for a moment, looking at each other with our mouths open. It didn't take more than a minute, but we simultaneously and silently agreed that this was the neatest thing since the ponytail. Wide-eyed and grinning, we tried it again. *Whoosh!* Again, tiny pieces of foam rubber shot about three feet up in the air, as if a geyser had erupted from the inside of the pillow. By then, completely out of control and unconcerned with the consequences, we started stabbing our pencils into the pillow over and over again, until it looked like a bizarrely localized blizzard had fallen in the unfinished basement. After another few minutes and about a hundred punctures later, the foam quit springing from the pillow and it had stopped making that wonderful *whooshing* sound.

We looked at each other in disappointment, as we briefly imagined that the fun had ended. But then, again simultaneously, the thought occurred to us that three more perfectly good pillows sat beside us just waiting to be impaled, and the fun started all over again. The first puncture was the mother lode: it made the loudest and most impressive *whooshing* sound, and the foam shot up the farthest and the fastest. We giggled and laughed, pointing at each other and laughing harder. Little tiny pieces of foam rubber covered every strand of our hair. I don't know what I looked like, but Tara looked like she had just come in from that oddly localized blizzard and the snow had not yet begun melting. The little white nodules evenly coated her hair and eyelashes. We experienced the most fun we had ever had in our young lives, until Grandma Grace snuck downstairs to see what in the world tickled us so.

I can confirm that neither Tara nor I could sit down for the rest of the day, and not for very long on the next. I also believe that my memories of that day have helped me make more informed decisions as a parent. I can still vividly remember the fun Tara and I experienced that day, but not once did I stop to realize that we were destroying those pillows. Of course, afterwards, I felt ashamed and embarrassed that I didn't realize the consequences of my actions (not to mention a mighty bit sore in my nether regions). Thinking back on it, the pillow incident has helped me put some of my own children's actions into perspective, understanding the result of some actions are unintentional. To hear Grandma Grace tell it, she was so angry that she came back and spanked us a second time. I don't remember that part, so evidently I didn't think the second lashing was undeserving—or maybe my butt had become too numb by then to feel it much. Grandma Grace said she felt guilty for spanking us that second time, although she never replaced the destroyed TV pillows. From that day forward, Tara and I sat on the sadly deflated ones with pencil holes all over them when we watched television. My guess is that the constant reminder of our deeds that day was our real punishment, in the justifiable hope that we wouldn't go for an encore.

One thing that I loved about living on the farm was that we could have all the animals that we desired. As a child, and even now as an adult, I love all animals. One fine evening, a man that Dad worked with came by with five Beagle puppies. He lived in the city and didn't have any place to keep them, but knew we didn't have a shortage of open space on the farm. We already had one dog, Snapper, but Mom let us keep the Beagle puppies, and we immediately picked out our favorite two, enamored by the fact that we each could have our own puppy. We promptly insisted that Mom pick out her favorite too, compelled to make sure every puppy had a responsible party. After she chose from the remaining three, Tara and I, in our ultimate wisdom, decided that it was only fair that Dad should be the proud owner of the other two, after all, he was the biggest of the family and as such, should have the most responsibility. I named my puppy Princess, and she became my new best friend. She had several annoying habits that I considered adorable but irritated the rest of the gang, humans and dogs alike. One of her perpetual routines consisted of lying in the dogs' food bowl while eating. The other beagles would run in circles around the dish, trying to inch their mouths close to the few morsels that lay uncovered around the edge. I thought it resembled the Keystone Cops, as they knocked each other down in the efforts to find the perfect opening. The other annoying habit that she had was to lay behind the rear car tire, escaping the heat of the summer sun while taking her many daily naps. Mom and Dad always searched behind the tires before they left in the vehicle, making sure Princess wasn't lounging behind one of them. Unfortunately one morning, Mom left late for work and in her haste, forgot to check for Princess and backed over her. Although very upset, at least we still had Snapper and the remaining gaggle of four Beagle puppies, which Dad graciously agreed to giving me my pick of his two, making the wound heal less painfully.

One day, the local dogcatcher came by the farm and couldn't help but notice that we had four unruly Beagle puppies running pell-mell through our yard. Snapper, perhaps sensing potential danger, just happened to be out carousing somewhere in the surrounding farmlands. None of our dogs had licenses, because we lived in the country, and frankly, Mom and Dad couldn't afford it. But this man insisted that the dogs required tags and proceeded to write Mom a ticket for the fees.

He turned to Mom and said, "Okay, so all you have is four dogs, correct?" Mom said yes, nodding her head. But Tara immediately piped up and added innocently, "And Snapper!" Mom just stood there silently, giving Tara the evil eye. The gentleman looked up and said, "Let me ask the question again. You have four dogs. You don't have any other dogs that aren't here right now." Mom said, carefully, "That's correct." Tara again leaned in precociously and blurted, "And Snapper!" I watched the incident not really understanding the true meaning of the encounter, but I knew that the time had come for Tara to shut up. The dogcatcher finished writing the ticket, eyeing Mom suspiciously, and left. Mom thought for sure that the guy would return again, looking for the missing Snapper, but he never did; the guy probably felt sorry for her having to feed so many animals plus raise two obnoxious children.

That Easter, following our move to the country, the Easter Bunny decided to bring Tara and me baby ducklings again. Of course, the fact of the matter is that Dad had to replace the ducks that he and Eddy had accidentally drowned the year before (I am sure both Dad and Eddy got the Mom-patented lecture one more time). The excitement of having a new little duckling, soft with downy fuzz and ever-so-delicate, overcame me, and I started jumping up and down. Dad hated it when I became that wound up, but I just couldn't help it and began hopping around like a deranged jackrabbit, expelling all of my pent-up energy. Although we hadn't had our previous ducks very long, we had been with them long enough to know we'd love to have more.

Alas, the ducklings weren't very old when the neighbor's dog ate Tara's duck. I don't know how mine survived, but he did. I named him Quacky, since he strutted around the yard, making quacking sounds. (Funny how we were in the habit of naming animals after their verbal communication skills. Heck, if I had a pet frog it would have been named Ribbit and we would have really been in trouble trying to come up with a name for a pet turtle!) I've heard it said that, if you have only one pet, then the pet, whether it's a cat, dog, or other animal, doesn't know that it's an animal. The logic behind this is pretty basic: if people are the only other creatures the animal interacts with, then it thinks it is a person too. At the time we got Quacky not only did we still have the four beagles, we also had Snapper who was a Heinz 57, as Dad called him. (I thought that a Heinz 57 was actually a breed of dog, and felt it was rather strange when people would laugh when they asked what type of dog Snapper was and I replied that he was a Heinz 57. I didn't see the humor in it myself; their amusement puzzled me, ignorant as I was to Dad's little joke.) While the Beagles spent their days amusing each other, Quacky and Snapper got along famously, and so Quacky spent 90 percent of his time running around with Snapper. The result, as you could have guessed by using the logic mentioned above, was that Quacky clearly thought he belonged to the canine family. Snapper barked at everything, so Quacky quacked at everything. Quacky refused to eat duck food, subsisting solely on dog food (Purina Dog Chow was his favorite), and Snapper and Quacky both slept in the doghouse together. They quickly became best friends.

Snapper was an old, experienced farm dog while Quacky was just a young duckling punk. Quacky obviously looked up to Snapper and eagerly wanted to learn the ropes about farm life. For example, Quacky found it very interesting any time a car drove by the house. The gravel road, elevated slightly above the yard level, created a mini-culvert of semi-hidden grass. Snapper, being the old, seasoned veteran of the farm, would crouch down in the culvert alongside the road whenever he heard a car approaching. The second the car passed our yard, Snapper would launch himself from his stationary position, barking furiously and running full bore after the car. For a couple of months, Quacky observed this ritual from the front yard with his head tilted inquisitively, now positively fascinated by Snapper's amusing pastime. We should have known, once Quacky started eating nothing but dog chow and commenced to sleeping in the dog house, that he might just get a head full of ideas eccentric for a duck.

Out in the country, sound travels for miles. Very few cars passed by our house, maybe one or two a day, but when they did, before you could even see the dust rising from the gravel road, you could hear them. Well, on this particular day, when Snapper positioned himself on one side of the road, Quacky covertly hid on the other. Just like a child who couldn't wait to the count of ten before peeking, Quacky would periodically pop his head up, straining and swiveling his neck, on the lookout for any sign of a passing vehicle. Then, just as quickly, he would snap his neck back down, as if he were a soldier in the jungle hiding from the enemy. He resembled a feathery periscope. Then, he began to nervously shift his weight between his two little webbed feet, back and forth, side to side, as if searching for the perfect balance. His little tail feathers wiggled impatiently as he positioned his body for the most precise angle of attack.

At long last, a car approached, thick tension and anticipation filled the air. Just at the right moment, the very second the car passed between them, up they sprang! Snapper ran with all his might, barking his fool head off and nipping at the car. Quacky, too, joined the chase. His sprinted wildly on his two little webbed feet, flapping his wings and quacking loudly all the while, darting his head towards the car as if to ward off an evil spirit. If this sight wasn't hilarious enough, the expressions on the passengers' faces as they drove by perfected the picture. People may expect dogs to chase cars out in the country, but no one expects to see a possessed duck flailing madly after them, trying with all his tiny might to intimidate a car.

When we moved away from the farm, we couldn't take Quacky or the Beagles. Fortunately, Mom and Dad knew a family that had a pond, about half a dozen ducks, and plenty of property to house the clan. Even though the thought of leaving my animals left me just this side of heartbroken, Mom and Dad convinced me that the arrangement would work out perfectly for the animals, especially Quacky, since once he figured out he was a duck, he could live a safer life. Dad dropped him off and we moved on to the city. A couple of weeks later Dad talked to Quacky's new owner, who told Dad that Quacky wouldn't have anything to do with the other ducks. He just sat on the side of the road waiting for cars to drive by.

Tragically but of course inevitably, Quacky eventually got run over by a car. My heart did break then, but I only shed a single tear.

I knew that Quacky died doing something that he loved. To this day, I choose to think he went to dog heaven, where I am convinced there are an over-abundance of cars driving down gravel roads just begging to be chased.

No More Green Acres

When I was six years old, we moved back to town. Mom and Dad purchased a newly built house in New Albany, on Mary Ann Drive. The street number was 2405, and I loved the fact that our address rhymed: 2405 Mary Ann Drive. It had three bedrooms, so for the first time in our lives, Tara and I had our own rooms, which delighted us. As well, we were excited to live in a neighborhood with other children. After spending our early years on the farm with very few neighbors within shouting distance, the concept of meeting new friends exhilarated us.

Our house in New Albany had a fairly large backyard, which we considered spacious enough to accommodate Snapper. We didn't have a fence, though, so we had to restrain Snapper with a chain. Snapper had never been chained up in his life, which felt drastically different to him. He had roamed the countryside at will when we lived on the farm, and in our new place, he remained confined to a city lot.

We hadn't lived in town very long before the mailman started complaining to Mom about Snapper. Snapper came by his name honestly: he barked at everything, loudly and fiercely, which tended to intimidate people who didn't know him. The mailman told Mom that Snapper had chased him the previous day and nipped at his ankles. He threatened to call the appropriate officials and report it. Mom claimed that it couldn't have been Snapper, as he lay in the backyard, still on his chain. She said, "Buddy, all I can say is if that is true, he's a damn smart dog. He must have removed his chain, chased you down the street, returned home and put his chain back on." The mailman refused to listen to her logic, adamantly claiming that Snapper was the offender, but Mom just ignored him. Still, to be safe, she decided to confine Snapper to the garage the next day when she left for work.

When she returned home that evening, she saw that Snapper remained in the garage; he clearly couldn't have been the perpetrator in any incident that might have happened that day. Again, the mailman stopped by and continued complaining about Snapper. Mom told him what she had done, and repeated her earlier sentiments, "Buddy, that must be a very smart dog indeed if he can unlock the garage door, chase you down the street, return home and lock the door behind himself." The undeterred mailman felt certain that Snapper was his persistent assailant. The next day when Mom turned into the neighborhood, just two blocks from home, she viewed Snapper sniffing one of our neighbor's garbage cans. She couldn't believe her eyes. She pulled the car over to the curb, and while leaving the car running, got out and yelled, "Snapper! What are you doing!?" In his ever so boisterous nature, Snapper started barking at her. Not amused, Mom walked over and opened the back door to the car and shouted, "Get in this car right now and shut up!" Snapper hesitated, knowing he was in trouble, but obediently entered the vehicle, situating himself in a sitting position in the middle of the back seat. For the few minutes it took Mom to drive home and pull into the driveway, she continually lectured Snapper about his wayward behavior, threatening to put a padlock on his chain. When they exited the vehicle and Mom marched him to the back yard, she nearly collapsed in shock to see the real Snapper lying next to his dog house, curious to see who Mom had brought home. The delinquent canine that Mom encountered on her journey home wasn't Snapper at all, but practically identical in size and color. Mom promptly released Snapper's twin and watched him as he ran off to find other avenues of mischief. Mom relayed the story of the brief dog-napping to the mailman, who chuckled, relieved to know he wasn't losing his mind. Snapper's name had been cleared.

Although we loved Snapper very much, he did not appreciate being chained up or locked in the garage. He yearned to roam the fields and farmlands of southern Indiana. Eventually, we could no longer endure Snapper's unhappiness, so our neighbors back at the farm adopted Snapper, where he lived to the ripe old age of fifteen. For Tara and me, that ended the wistful era of owning pets bigger than a breadbox—until we grew up and left home, that is. I believe our farm rearing sealed our fate of being animal lovers. Tara and I longed for cute and furry companions, who always loved and accepted us, no matter what the situation. When we released Snapper back to the wilderness of farm life, it left a void in both of us that would end up not getting filled until much later in life. Not to say that we didn't try a lot of substitutions along the way.

A few months later on a visit to the local department store, Mom went off to do the necessary shopping while I loitered in the pet department. I took pleasure in watching the fish, a habit I picked up from Grandma Grace. She kept a fish tank full of mollies and minnows. I think she started with two of each, which multiplied into hundreds, swimming around and around in her five-gallon tank. The adults used to chuckle about it, and always made reference to rabbits, which I didn't understand what fish and rabbits could possibly have in common. Regardless, I spent many peaceful hours just watching the fish gracefully migrate around the tank.

On that particular day as I wasted time in the pet department, I happened upon the golden hamsters. They looked cute and soft and furry, and I wanted one so badly my teeth ached. As a bonus, the store ran a special deal that day: if you purchased a cage and a water bottle, you received the hamster free. It sounded like the deal of a lifetime to me, and Mom didn't have the heart to say no, not after she forced us to bid farewell to our best friend Snapper after moving to town. I promised to clean the cage regularly and make sure my hamster got properly fed. The cage at the store housed six or seven hamsters, and I insisted on holding each one before deciding which one I wanted. They all looked similar, but some of them seemed more nervous than others. I selected one that moved calmly, and I could tell he really liked me, so we took him home to our house on Mary Ann Drive. I named him Hammy, which deviated slightly from our previous method of naming pets, although hamsters don't make a lot of sound, normally.

However, Mom wouldn't let me keep Hammy in my room. She didn't allow pets with fur in the house, at least not the part of the house that we lived in. She wouldn't even allow us to keep dust bunnies under our beds. Luckily, our house had a full, unfinished basement on the bottom level. Mom kept the washer and dryer down there, in addition to numerous boxes full of belongings that we would probably never use again but just couldn't bear to part with. Natural wood stairs led down to the basement's cement floor and concrete walls lined the outer perimeter. An old chest of drawers sat in the corner of the basement, which seemed like the perfect place for Hammy's new home. We prepared his cage with the essentials and placed Hammy and his new home on top of the dresser. Hammy appeared satisfied with his new surroundings, and personally, I felt elated to have a new friend to care for.

The only bad thing about the arrangement was that I always became a little spooked when I went downstairs alone. The narrow windows in the basement measured only about a foot high and a couple of feet wide. The windows appeared at the very top of the basement walls. As a result, the basement always appeared dimly lit, even in the middle of the day. Several steel poles protruded from the base of the cement floor that supported the ceiling of the basement (or technically the floor of the main living structure), placed about every ten feet or so. The furnace stood in the middle of the basement at the far end. From outside the house, the diminutive windows were at ground level, and even though they had locks on them, I feared that an intruder would get in somehow and conceal himself behind the furnace. Every time I went down stairs, the first thing that I did was peek around the furnace to make sure that no one lurked behind it. Then I checked Hammy's food and water, and played with him. Sometimes I went downstairs and roller-skated while I talked to him. I always felt a bit silly that I was so uneasy about going down to the basement. I believed that I was the only person who feared that a stranger might invade our sanctuary, until an occurrence decisively confirmed that other people in the house also contemplated the possibility.

One night while the family slept, Mom heard an unusual noise. She didn't recognize it, but it sounded like a dull thud, as if something struck a piece of wood, or stepped on a wooden floor with hard-soled shoes. As she lay there motionless, straining to hear the faintest of sounds, she heard it again. She turned to Dad, who slept beside her, and whispered his name. Out of his mouth came a tense "Ssshhhh," which indicated that he had heard it too. Every hair on Mom's body immediately stood at attention. Mom expected Dad's response to be, "Go back to sleep, it's nothing." Instead, knowing that Dad equally shared her concern, she grew even more frightened. Then, the sound repeated again. It sounded like someone slowly climbed the basement stairs, as if to avoid detection. Dad shot out of bed and made a beeline to the basement door. Mom raced out the front door and ran next door to our neighbor's house. She banged on their front door and screamed, "Eddy Joe! Eddy Joe! Come quick! Someone is in our basement!" Seconds later, Eddy Joe flew out his front door, wearing nothing but a pair of boxer shorts and carrying a shotgun. That had to have been an unsightly spectacle, and I'm glad I slept so soundly that I missed that particular excitement. Eddy Joe was a very large man, and as a child, I felt in awe of the size of his belly. He would have made a great Santa Claus, and he certainly didn't need any extra padding.

Eddy Joe charged through the front door, through the living room and the kitchen, and ran to the basement door. Dad, also clad only in boxer shorts, crept down the stairs first and paused, listening for any sound. Again, the sound rang out. Thud. Pause. Thud. It sounded as if it originated from the far end of the basement, from right behind the furnace. The two brave men charged down the stairs and around the furnace, one man approaching from the left, the other from the right. When they met up on the other side, they could immediately see that no intruder crouched behind the furnace, and they both stood there puzzled, looking at each other. Then it happened again. Thud! The sound emanated directly behind them, and as they slowly turned around, they observed Hammy pawing at his water bottle. It had fallen off the side of the cage and lay on top of the chest of drawers. Each time the hamster pushed on the top of the mouthpiece, the bottle rose slightly off the top of the dresser. Eventually, his grip would fail, and the bottle would drop back down onto the dresser, making a dull thudding sound. I can only imagine the sight of two grown men in boxer shorts, still wide-eyed and panting from fear-induced adrenaline, staring down at a thirsty little hamster. Dad reattached Hammy's water bottle, thanked Eddy Joe for his assistance, and then decided to try to get some more sleep. Although I don't imagine the adults got much of it the rest of the night.

One thing that Tara and I have always had in common is that neither one of us enjoys getting up in the morning. It has nothing to do with enduring a sleepless night; we just have a difficult time waking up in the morning. As a child, I loved Saturday mornings because we slept as late as we wanted. In fact, sometimes I woke up disappointed because I had slept so late that I missed most of the cartoons on television. Since we attended church on Sunday, Saturday was the only day we got to sleep late, and thus, it quickly became our favorite day of the week.

The rest of the week, we rose at the crack of dawn. During the school year, Monday through Friday, Tara and I had to ride the bus to school, which meant we had to get up when told and scurry about in order to catch the bus on time. As the obedient child, I jumped out of bed, even if woefully sleepy, and got ready when Mom told me to. Always aware of the rules, especially Mom's rules (you know: the sacred tablets), not to mention the consequences of breaking them, I did my best to follow them. Tara, on the other hand, consistently pushed rules to the limit. Every morning as I dressed for school, I heard Mom in Tara's room telling her to get out of bed. This happened three or four times every morning before Tara's feet actually made contact with the floor. It puzzled me as to why she didn't just get up the first time. I didn't like getting in trouble or being yelled at, so I simply did as I was told. As a result, every morning after getting dressed and ready to go, I had to wait for Tara to finish up so that we could leave for the bus stop.

One morning she procrastinated a few minutes too long, and as we approached the bus stop, we caught sight of the bus driving away. We waved our arms and yelled, but the driver didn't see us, or at least he pretended not to. Tara knew she would be reprimanded because she didn't get out of bed in time if we went home to tell Mom, so we decided to walk to school. I was only seven years old at the time, and the school was a few miles away, but we knew how to get there. We had ridden the bus for almost a year at that point and had become very familiar with the route. Thus, we also knew that we would have to walk briskly in order to arrive at school on time.

It never occurred to me that this would create a problem. I didn't want to upset Mom, who had probably already left for work. I didn't see any other alternative but to walk. It actually sounded like a fine adventure to me, and Tara definitely didn't want to have to tell Mom we missed the bus. We actually had a great time that morning walking to school. As we walked, the cool spring breeze rippled through our skirts and tickled our legs. We talked about the approaching summer and our expectations of what we might encounter. It was silly chatter, two school girls giggling at the other one's bantering. We lost track of time and reality, as we enjoyed the freedom of no one being in charge. We imagined being drifters, looking for the next approaching train and speculating where our next destination would be.

I have no idea how long it took us to get there, but as we approached the school grounds, I thought it would facilitate our arrival if we got on the same side of the road as the school. Tara said that wasn't a good idea, because pedestrians always walked facing on-coming traffic. I knew that, but since we approached within a couple hundred feet of the school and there wasn't any traffic, I crossed the road. Of course, when we got to the school grounds, a few of the teachers and the principal stood outside looking anxious, watching us walk up to the school, with no other students in sight. Suddenly, I experienced a feeling of dread wash over me. I thought once we arrived at school, all the other kids would be out in front, and we would blend right in. I didn't expect anyone would notice how we got there. I can assure you that we didn't blend in that day. In fact, I'm pretty sure we were the last two children to arrive at school that morning.

The authorities at the school called Mom when the school bus arrived, absent Tara and me. For the twenty or so minutes after the bus arrived and Tara and I continued our careless jaunt to the school grounds, Mom had visions of our faces being profiled on a milk carton. Of course, her horror quickly turned to parental anger after she realized we had arrived unharmed. Although relieved that we had arrived to school safely, we received a lecture from both the principal and Mom about our choices that day. I felt totally humiliated that I had to go to the principal's office. I know Tara feared Mom more than the principal, but back then, the parents allowed principals to deliver lickings when appropriate. As you might suspect, Mom and

Dad's signed consent remained on file, so we received our share of punishment from both the principal and Mom on that day. But it all worked out fine in the end – that is, after we could sit back down.

As Tara grew older and became more head strong, commonly Mom and Tara bickered. They didn't see eye-to-eye on most issues. Mom was pretty restrictive—some people might call her overprotective—but I tend to believe that she just tried to be a smart parent. One particular day that Tara wanted to do something that Mom disagreed with, Tara decided that she would run away from home. Tara couldn't have been more than eight years old at the time. Mom told her that if she seriously wanted to leave home, she needed some essentials to take with her. Mom dug up an old broomstick from the garage, took one of Dad's handkerchiefs and crafted Tara a hobo pack for her journey. She put her toothbrush inside and made Tara a sandwich, just in case she got hungry. Grabbing her bundle hastily, Tara went out the front door in a huff. Mom stood back in the shadows and observed her out the front window where Tara couldn't see her. Tara trudged up to the corner, only two houses away, and began pacing back and forth. Tara's attention vacillated between what lay down the street and her secure home, just two houses away. Then she resumed pacing back and forth, as if undecided as to what she should do. Eventually, she sat down, opened her knapsack, took out her sandwich and ate it. After about thirty minutes, Mom walked up to the corner and said, "Tara, what are you doing? I thought you wanted to run away from home." Tara responded tearfully in an angry tone, "How am I supposed to run away from home when I can't even cross the street?" One of Mom's rules was that we could not venture farther than the corner and we couldn't cross the main road that our subdivision sat next to. A flurry of constant traffic filled the street and Mom didn't want us to get hit by a car. So Tara just sat at the corner, not knowing what to do, since Mom had banned her from crossing the busy street.

Speaking of Mom's rules, another thing she forbade us to do when we moved to Mary Ann Drive was to ride our bikes on the street. Because our street followed a circular pattern off the main road, the only traffic on our road originated from the people who resided on Mary Ann Drive, except for an occasional visit from the mailman and the ice cream man. You can imagine just how often a car drove down our street: rarely. Nevertheless, for some reason only Mom could fathom, she did not allow us to ride our bikes on the street. All the other kids rode their bikes on the street, and sometimes Tara and I would race them. We would tear down the sidewalk, while the other kids would zoom up on the street. The other parents looked unkindly upon Tara and I riding our bikes on the sidewalk, as it would sometimes inconvenience them—not to mention scare the pants off of them—when they went out to pick up their mail or their newspaper. God knows we didn't always ride our bikes in complete control. But Mom remained firm on the issue—that is, until the inevitable happened, and Tara ran right over a little girl on roller skates. Tara didn't see her coming and hit her with her bike, knocking the poor girl to the ground. When the girl got back on her feet, crying, with her elbows and knees scratched and bleeding, Tara knew she was in trouble. Interestingly enough, though, Mom didn't get angry, and the next thing we knew, she allowed us to ride our bikes on the street. It was uncanny how Tara's misfortunate accident coincided with our new-found privileges. I guess the other parents decided to gang up on Mom since they felt their children were in perpetual jeopardy of getting assaulted by out-of-control bikers on the sidewalk.

It's fun to look back at our antics as children, even if the choices resulted in embarrassment or possibly a slight form of humiliation. Sometimes misfortune doesn't result in a bad ending, and at times, no matter what you do it seems some things are just meant to be. The Butterfly Effect comes to mind. If Tara or I had changed one thing in our young lives or made one different choice along the way, would the world be worse off? Probably not, but I know I wouldn't change anything in my past, for fear that I might leave out something important, no matter how insignificant it may seem today. Though occasionally I think about the little girl on the roller skates and wonder if she feels the same way.

Drive-in Addicts

My preference for horror films developed at an early age. Grandma Grace loved horror films and a drive-in movie theatre sat just around the corner from where she lived in New Albany, Indiana. Because Tara and I spent a lot of time at Grandma Grace's house during our early years, we became repeatedly exposed to the Friday night triple feature of horror films. As a young child, the films scared the wits out of me, but when Grandma Grace asked us if we wanted to go to the drive-in, Tara and I always said yes, of course, because we loved going anywhere, especially to the movies.

Grandma Grace never learned to drive, because she didn't feel the need to. Grandpa Willard or Uncle Wayne drove her anywhere that she needed or wanted to go. So when Grandma Grace decided to treat us to a drive-in movie, usually Uncle Wayne got the dubious honor of driving us. The first couple of times we experienced the sheer terror of these films, I couldn't sleep a wink. But, with each subsequent viewing, the movies became less and less frightening. Eventually, Grandma Grace's love of horror movies rubbed off on both Tara and me. Even today, I love a movie that grabs your attention at the beginning and doesn't let go until the credits start rolling. I guess it started with movies, but these days I love a good horror book as well, and Stephen King is my idol. But I'll tell you more about that later.

Mom and Dad used to take us to the drive-in, too, every once in a while. With our parents, we mostly went to see Elvis Presley films, but Tara and I didn't really care what movie played on the big screen. We just loved going to the movies, eating popcorn and staying up late. There was a playground at the drive-in, as well, that sat right in front of the base of the big screen. It had a swing set, a teeter-totter, and a slide. Mom always allowed Tara and me to visit the playground if we arrived at the drive-in early, despite the fact that Tara and I dressed in our pajamas before we left for the drive-in so that when we returned home, asleep in the back seat, Dad could carry us straight to bed. Dressed in our house slippers and pajamas, without a care in the world, Tara and I played on the swings and teeter-totter before the projector started rolling.

Fond of gadgets, one year Dad bought a rain guard for the windshield, made especially for use at the drive-in theater. It consisted of a plastic cover that connected to the top of the car with suction cups and extended to the front part of the hood. Two poles with rubber, suction-cupped feet attached to the hood of the car and prevented the rain from falling on the windshield. At the time, Tara and I thought we owned the most sophisticated scientific invention ever, because if it rained, Dad didn't have to run the windshield wipers which invariably ruined a good drive-in movie, since blurred faces appeared between each swipe of the wipers. We felt privileged to have the shield, and surprisingly, it worked pretty well. So good, in fact, that Dad bought a second one. We had a blue one and a red one. Don't ask me why Dad suspected we would ever need more than one, but having two did offer us a choice of colors. Myself, I preferred the blue one.

The highlight of going to the drive-in theatre in New Albany—better than the playground, even better than the movie most times—was the raffle. Before the movie started, everyone put their name in a box in the concession stand. At a designated time prior to the start of the evening's features, the people who worked at the drive-in drew a name out of the hopper. Whoever's name was drawn won a pony. Tara wanted a pony so badly her teeth ached. Every time we went to the drive-in, we stood inside the concession area and listened with tingling anticipation as they announced the winner of the drawing. Time after time, we left disappointed, Tara blowing out a huff of exasperated air, until one fateful night. Miracle of miracles, Tara's name finally got drawn.

The drive-in kept about a dozen ponies in a field that lay adjacent to the drive-in theatre, so the very next day we went to pick up our pony. The owners didn't just let you select your pony of choice and deliver it, because that would be too easy. Instead, the winning person had to corral and catch the pony, then figure out how the heck to get it home. In our case, that person just happened to be Dad, since Tara was not yet big enough to catch a pony on her own. I still remember the look of shock and horror mingled on Dad's face when the guy handed him the rope and said, "Get whichever one you want." By the size of the grin on the gentleman's face, apparently he enjoyed watching the winners attempt to secure a rope around their selected specimen. Dad turned to Tara and asked her which one she preferred. Tara selected a shiny, black pony with an attitude. Dad entered the fenced area and slowly approached the pony. Obviously, Dad thought if he moved calmly the horse would not become startled. But every time Dad got any closer than a ten-foot radius around the pony, the equine threw up his head and nickered as he ran away, mocking Dad's feeble attempts to capture him. After a couple of hours and long after Dad's patience ran out, he successfully placed a rope around the neck of Tara's new pony.

We didn't have a horse trailer or any vehicle in which to haul a pony, other than Grandpa Alfred's pickup truck, which wasn't the safest alternative in the world, as you can imagine. Regardless, Dad borrowed Grandpa Alfred's pickup truck, which had wooden slats above the truck bed. Typically, Alfred used the truck to take the corn he grew to the market; the wooden slats allowed him to stack the corn above the top of the truck bed. Clearly, it wasn't designed to haul a pony, but thankfully, the truck proved to be the experienced and durable work-horse Alfred built.

Tara named her pony Fancy, and we ended up taking him to Grandpa Alfred and Grandma Nola's farm. We spent every weekend, mainly Sundays, visiting the grandparents, so we got to see Fancy every Sunday after church. When we first brought Fancy home, no one could get close to him. Tara hung on the fence and begged Fancy to come over to her. She pleaded, "Fancy, I love you. Come here, boy, come here. I love you." Fancy just stared at Tara like she was from another planet. After several Sundays of this, we decided that the only way that we were going to get any use out of Fancy was to get a saddle on him and ride him. So we gave Dad our precious silver dollar collection, and he went out and purchased a saddle and a bridle.

Unlike Tara, I didn't possess a strong love for horses or ponies, because I preferred animals that were smaller than me. A few days later, Dad thought it would be a wonderful surprise for Tara if we saddle-broke Fancy while Tara attended school. After Tara got on the school bus, Dad and I headed for the farm, and when we about halfway there, he decided to let me in on his plan. My heart rate immediately accelerated with fear. I could think of a hundred different things that I would rather do that morning than get on a pony with a bad attitude, one that had never even seen a saddle, let alone have one on its back. But as usual, I didn't get to vote on the issue. Once we arrived and as Dad cinched up the belt around Fancy's belly, preparing him for training, I continually pleaded with Dad not to make me get on Fancy's back. If Tara had been there, she would have pushed me out of the way to be first in the saddle. But unfortunately, in Tara's absence and knowing that Fancy was too small for an adult to ride, so I didn't have an alternative case to plea.

Dad lifted me onto the saddle and proceeded to adjust the stirrups until they hung at the proper length. I felt my body trembling as I grasped the yoke of the saddle as tight as I possibly could. I observed Fancy's mane begin to shake as his skin shivered, and the shudder rippled down his neck, across his back, and down the end of his tail.

As the tip caught the last of the quiver, he flicked his tail up and hit me squarely in the back of the head. The impact stung, like a well-directed whip and the back of my skull started burning at the point of contact. Fancy lunged forward and a long squeal escaped my lips, manifesting itself into a five-second form of "Daaaaaaaaaaaaaaaad", who assured me that he had everything under control. Fancy didn't rare up, or buck as you might suspect a normal pony would behave through such an ordeal, but instead, that damn horse started hopping around like a friggin' bunny rabbit. Dad tripped on the lead rope, lost his footing and fell to the ground, losing his grip on the only lifeline I had. Fancy continued to hop, as if he had springs on his hooves, and I continued to squeal with each bounce. Dad scrambled to regain his footing, which was about the time I felt the saddle sliding sideways. I grasped Fancy's mane, trying to keep the saddle on the top of his back, but with every jump, the saddle slipped another couple of inches, until by body was perpendicular to the earth below. One final hop straight off the ground and my grip failed, sending me crashing to the ground.

I didn't attempt to get up, but just lay there thankful to have survived the whole encounter. Fancy didn't run but instead stood still, turned his head to look back at me and nickered, flipping his tail in victory. Dad ran over and grabbed the bridle as I continued to lie on the ground, attempting to soothe my bruised pride and waiting for my heart beat to return to normal. Dad calmly looked at me and asked, "Are you alright?" When I rose to my feet, the tears started rolling as I brushed the dirt off my clothes, and replied in frustration, "Yeah, but why can't we just have normal animals?" Dad inquired, "What do you mean?" I said, "First we have a duck that thinks he's a dog and now we have a pony that thinks he's a rabbit!" Dad tried to stifle a smile, but as he shrugged his shoulders I could see the controlled stiffness of his mouth loosen, giving way to a grin. At that point, I realized how comical the scene must have been with a crazed horse hopping up and down, and the giggles started. Dad said, "You did it!" I nodded my head and we stood in the dirt laughing, knowing that Fancy could now be ridden. Tara became extremely agitated when she arrived home from school that afternoon and discovered that I was the first one to ride Fancy. But it didn't take her long to get over it, realizing that Fancy could now be ridden every day, and she felt ecstatic! Frankly, I couldn't wait for her to try him out, wanting to be the witness instead of the participant, and she did, but not one single hop escaped Fancy's legs after Tara saddled up on him. Traitor!

Still, Fancy wasn't fond of his newly acquired chore of carrying kids around the farm. He always found the lowest branch on a tree to walk under, hoping to knock his rider off. He definitely had a mind of his own, and usually what he thought or wanted didn't coincide with what the person riding him thought or wanted. For her part, Tara behaved a bit like a tomboy and had her share of attitude as well. When Fancy knocked her off, she stood up, brushed herself off, and gave Fancy a right cross to the chin. Me, I decided that I wouldn't ride anymore and decided to pursue some safer activity, like walking the wrong way down a busy street blindfolded.

When we first brought Fancy to the farm, my grandfather put him in with the dairy cows, thinking that would give him some company. Horses and cows theoretically get along fine. But Fancy, being young and energetic, wanted to play, so he started chasing the dairy cows all over the place. This turned out to be disastrous for the farm revenue, because the more upset and worked up the cows became, the less milk they produced. As Fancy tried playing herd-boss to all the cows, my grandfather's livelihood became seriously compromised.

It quickly became apparent that the situation needed a resolution, so my grandfather moved Fancy into an empty pasture. Fancy didn't like being alone either, though, and he kept escaping from the pasture and running free on my grandfather's forty-acre farm. Every time Fancy escaped, the adults chased him down and put him back in the pasture, just to find him loose again later that same day. Fancy was pretty small, so we couldn't imagine that he was capable of jumping the fence, but, without evidence to the contrary, that seemed to be the only way Fancy repeatedly set himself free. Grandma Nola decided to conduct her own investigation into the problem, so she hid behind some bushes after Grandpa Alfred had yet again put Fancy back in his pasture and watched to see what the spirited pony would do. The fencing around the pasture consisted of livestock wire, a series of interlocking squares welded together, open in the center for air and light to pass through. As Grandma Nola quietly observed, Fancy carefully placed his hooves in between the squares and slowly, carefully climbed the fence. Grandma Nola could not believe her eyes—a horse climbing a fence! Who'd ever heard of such a thing? When Fancy got close to the top, probably four feet high, he kicked out his back hooves and launched himself over the fence. With the mystery finally solved, it quickly became clear that constraining Fancy to a designated area was a feat that might never successfully be achieved.

Obviously, Fancy was a mischievous instigator and an unusually clever animal, and not content to spend his days in quiet boredom. Instead, he spent his days looking for trouble. For example, Grandma Nola always hung her laundry out to dry on the clothesline, and one day, after painstakingly pinning up all the wet clothes, she glanced out of the window and observed Fancy systematically removing each item of clothing off the line. She ran out of the house, screaming her fool head off. Fancy had his mouth on her best petticoat at the time, and when he saw her coming, he tore off through the yard, but not before he managed to kick Nola's clothespin basket halfway across the lawn and into the flowerbed. Even though Grandma Nola stood only five feet tall, she had at least ten feet of determination. Still, although she made a valiant effort chasing Fancy and her best petticoat down that day, she couldn't quite catch him. So, that Sunday she had to dress for church without her best petticoat. In fact, it was almost time for the fall harvest before Grandpa Alfred stumbled upon the petticoat stuffed in the corner of the corncrib.

That was it for Fancy. Grandma Nola and Grandpa Alfred decided that they couldn't tolerate his antics any longer. After searching for someone to care for him, they found another family who agreed to take him, so he moved to a new farm. Tara lost it, of course. Mom was in the hospital at the time having one of her many surgeries, during which Tara experienced all the negative emotions known to mankind. She felt sad, angry, self-indulgent and hateful. Tara cried incessantly and Grace said, "You're not crying over that crazy pony, you're crying because your mother is in the hospital." Tara looked up at her and said, "I don't care about Mom being in the hospital. I don't care if she is sick or hurt or . . . or dead!" She sniffled miserably. "I want my pony back!" Tara played the role of drama queen to the hilt that day. Her heart ached and she wanted everyone else to share her pain and suffering. For me, though, Fancy was never my favorite animal anyway so I didn't get very upset. After all, he really belonged to Tara. I don't know whatever happened to Fancy, but I do know this: he was extremely lucky that, after all his shenanigans, he just got sent away to another farm and not to the factory to be renamed "Elmer."

Despite our rather rocky experience with Fancy, my love for the drive-in theater never diminished over time. Today, drive-ins are more or less a memory, and pretty close to extinct. I do know that as my boys grew up, my husband Robert and I took them to the drive-in every once in a while. It just wasn't the same, though. Now when you go to the drive-in, there is a radio channel that you tune into to hear the audio. Although the sound quality is much improved, it really takes the fun out of having to show up early and drive around to find the one speaker on the lot that works halfway decent. I'm sure the adults thought the hunt for a good speaker was a hassle, but as a child, it felt like going on an adventure. I remember feeling a sense of accomplishment when we found the best-sounding speaker smack dab in the middle of the lot in the perfect parking spot: not too close to the screen, so that Tara and I didn't have to lean forward to see the top of the movie through the windshield and not too far back from the screen, so that the picture looked sharp and the smallest of details could be seen from that distance. Finding that perfect spot with its nearly perfect speaker that didn't fade in and out or crackle and hiss with static: that was the ultimate in the drive-in experience. Life just didn't get any better than that.

Go West Young Man

While growing up in Indiana, our extended family expected that we would live there our entire lives, as our clan had planted and grown deep roots there. My father's parents lived there; my mother's parents lived there; and all of their siblings, my aunts and uncles, lived there. That was the expected thing to do. As children grew up, they got married, had a family and bought a house nearby. They stayed for the rest of their lives. As such, we developed a very close-knit family.

Nobody thought about the vast country that existed outside the small state of Indiana, at least not as a place of residence. The rest of the United States existed as exotic locations to visit while on vacation. Although true for everyone else in our family, Dad always insisted that you couldn't truly become acquainted with an area unless you lived there. His restless soul yearned to break the mold that had been cast by his parents and all those that came before him. Everyone always said that Dad had nomad blood in him, since he was not content to live out his days in the small Indiana community, the place that so many before him believed was the center of the universe.

When I was twelve years old, we lived in Columbus, Indiana. We had moved there two years prior. Columbus is only about 60 or 70 miles north of New Albany, but for my grandparents, they even considered that as leaving home—surely, they couldn't fathom that our minor relocation was merely the proverbial tip of the iceberg. As it inevitably came to pass, at the end of my sixth grade school year, Dad came home one day and announced that we were moving to Colorado. He had accepted a job offer and his new boss scheduled him to start work on Monday of the following week. Dad made his announcement on the Wednesday before. As I got older, I learned not to dwell too much on receiving short notice of a move. When you have nomad blood in you, it is not uncommon to have to cancel a doctor or dentist appointment because you will not be living in the same state at the time of said appointment, even if it was scheduled only a couple of days later.

I discovered our new plans—effective immediately—when I got home from school. Knowing how Tara, the drama queen in the family, would react, Mom went to her school that day to inform her of the news. They summoned Tara into the principal's office to let her know that this would be her last day. Tara became totally distraught, unsurprisingly. She started crying and didn't stop the rest of the day. She cried through every class, and as she commuted between classes, a constant stream of tears rolled down her cheeks. She passed one of her teachers later that day and her teacher stopped her and said, "Tara, what is wrong with you. Every time I've seen you today, you've been crying." Tara blurted out, "I'm moving and I don't want to leave my friends." Her teacher said, "Well, sometimes we have to do things we don't like. But take the time that you have left with your friends and make the best of it. There is still a couple of weeks left of school, so make them count." Tara turned to him and said, "No, you don't understand. Today is my last day here! My mom came up to school this morning to tell me." The instantly bewildered teacher didn't know how to respond. Obviously, he couldn't understand moving to another state with only one day's notice. But then again most people can't—most people not possessing a wanderer's heart, that is.

Mom took the news of the move in stride, after all, Mom and Dad eloped when they got married, briefly moving to Mississippi for the first year of their union. It was the first time she ventured from home. I guess after she agreed to that initial move, her pioneering spirit took hold. I believe she actually looked forward to the many spontaneous decisions Dad would make throughout their marriage. As such, Mom rented a U-haul truck later that day. We loaded everything we owned into the back of the truck and pulled out of town the very next morning. We didn't have another vehicle, as my father, who worked in the car business, always had company cars at his disposal; the U-haul became our sole means of transportation. We pulled out of the parking lot and headed towards the Great West. We knew what our goal was: "Pikes Peak or Bust" read the sign we secured on the back of the U-haul. I didn't really understand the meaning at the time. I got the Pikes Peak part, just not the Bust, and felt timid about asking what it meant. But other people must have gotten it, because many of them honked and waved as we drove by, as if wishing us good luck in our journey. I figured then that the phrase must be profound. Unlike Tara, I felt fairly excited about the move. Maybe Mom and Dad passed on a bit of their adventuresome spirits to me, or maybe I didn't fully grasp the reality of pulling up stakes and not looking back. Regardless, I had never really seen a mountain to speak of and had heard the Rocky Mountains were beautiful. I tried sitting still and not fidgeting, but had difficulty because the trip had just begun and the anticipation of the unknown quickened.

During our journey, we stopped in a town called Sharon Springs to get gas. A gentleman at the station conversed with Dad and said that we could take a shorter route that went straight to Colorado Springs, but we had to follow Prairie Road. I knew right then we might be in trouble: what is it about men and short cuts? The gas station attendant handed Dad a pamphlet that had a hand-drawn map of Prairie Road on it. All he had to say was *short cut*, and Dad already made up his mind. He had never laid eyes on this gentleman before, but they bonded instantly and built an immediate and mutual trust via that one simple phrase.

Dad had no trouble finding Prairie Road. We tooled down the two-lane road and felt pretty good about our trip. It was a beautiful day. Dad was happy (since he had found a *short cut*), and we felt mostly content (Tara had settled down a bit) to be embarking on another grand adventure. Suddenly, though, Dad started slowing down the unwieldy U-haul, and as we looked up the road a ways, it appeared that the road just . . . disappeared. Dad started shifting his weight around in his seat, indicating his nervousness and conveying that maybe he began to doubt his decision to take the alleged short cut. The part of the road we could see was completely covered with tumbleweed. We could also see another car in the on-coming lane on the other side of the tumbleweed, about 100 feet up the road. As we got closer we could see the road on the other side because the U-haul sat up high, allowing us a better view.

But I don't think the guy driving the vehicle on the other side could see if the road continued or just dropped off over a cliff. I can just imagine his thoughts as well, as he had probably encountered a gas station attendant who said, "Oh no, don't use the interstate. Here. Take this hand-drawn map and go down Prairie Road. You'll get there a lot quicker. It's a straight through shot. *Trust me.*" He might've trusted the attendant at first, but by this point, he probably thought, "Yeah, right. That guy might be a rocket scientist, but he certainly doesn't know Jack about the roads around here. This road isn't even finished!!" Anyway, Dad carefully maneuvered the truck, using the large bumper on the front to push the tumbleweed aside, clearing both lanes, so that the traffic could get through. The guy on the other side waved gratefully, conveying his thanks. (I think there was a little bonding going on there too, as both men must have been thinking, "Thank God this appears to be working out all right! I knew this *short cut* was a good idea!")

After a long day on the road, the sun began to set. Far off in the distance I could see the outline of the Rocky Mountains. As the sun went down and the sky grew darker, the landscape ahead appeared more and more ominous. The mountains' silhouette resembled a sleeping giant far off in the distance. Then, the peaks took on a purple hue and loomed gigantic and spooky. Despite my fascination with the changing mountain scenery, I noticed my stomach ached from hunger (not to mention the pangs from my overextended bladder), as we had not stopped for a while. It's that thing about men not wanting to stop more than once every 1,000 miles or until they need gas. Dad had said that we would stop in the next town to fill up and get something to eat. Oh, and to relieve ourselves, should we need to (Yeah, right! Like our eyeballs haven't already turned yellow!). Now, here's an indispensable piece of information you should jot down should you plan a trip across Kansas and Colorado on Highway 94: stop and get gas at Sharon Springs (and do whatever else you think you will need to do in the next five hours). There are very little facilities between there and Colorado Springs. I would even suggest taking a port-a-potty if you can manage it, unless you have a bladder made of cast iron. And don't, and I mean DON'T drink anything after getting back in the car at Sharon Springs. If you do, it could be painful.

As the madman behind the wheel tried to squeeze every single minute out of the drive he could, frenetically ticking off the miles, I started to get more than a little hungry. Suddenly and quite surprisingly, I smelled the aroma of bacon, lettuce, and tomato sandwiches. I sat there for a minute, thinking that maybe I was dying of starvation and had lapsed into wild hallucinations. Pausing with my nose in the air, sniffing timidly, I became convinced: I wasn't going crazy; I knew I could smell bacon, lettuce, and tomato sandwiches. So I mentioned it to Mom, Dad, and Tara, who seemed as surprised as I, but then Mom said she thought she could smell them too. I scanned the countryside out the window for any sign of a restaurant, but only dusty prairie and desert surrounded us. Tara and I sat in the middle between Mom and Dad, and Tara surreptitiously nudged me and whispered, "Shhh, I farted." I thought she was acting silly and trying to make me laugh, to distract me from my ravenous desire for those sandwiches, but I felt bound and determined that I was going to find that restaurant where we could stop and eat. So I repeated myself again, and insisted, "I smell bacon, lettuce, and tomato sandwiches." Weirdly, Tara blushed and squirmed in her seat. What I didn't realize was that Tara was slowly dying of embarrassment because she had tried to sneak one out: you know, a SBD, a Silent, But Deadly fart. Unknowingly, I made sure that everyone in the car noticed. Embarrassingly, I thought it smelled pretty good, which should give you some idea of just how hungry I had become. Finally, in total humiliation, Tara confessed. She said, "Okay, *fine*. I *farted*. I thought about eating bacon sandwiches, and I farted!! Now it smells like bacon, lettuce, and tomato sandwiches!" Obviously, her stomach ached with hunger too, but her newly professed talent had never been revealed to me before—an ability to transmit thought through gas. "Quite impressive", I thought. Disappointed about the nonexistent restaurant, but nonetheless impressed by her alchemical abilities.

We all got a pretty good chuckle out of it, hungry or not. Actually, Mom and Dad thought it was pretty hilarious, though Tara still cringed from embarrassment, and I felt positively broken-hearted that there wasn't a restaurant in the area. Dad started nervously asking about the mileage on the map. According to him, we were good for another 20 miles or so, but we needed gas sometime in the very near future. Of course, the only point of reference that we had was a hand-drawn pamphlet/map and we depended solely on the talismanic properties of the *short cut*. Back then, it seems, the road on which we travelled was not on the Rand McNally map (that should have been our first hint that—perhaps, just perhaps—there might not be a lot of services available on that stretch of road and—maybe, just maybe— it might not be such a good idea to take your entire family and everything you own on this particular route in the dark). Going west from Sharon Springs, the map showed a dot called Punkin Center and then a bigger dot called Rush. Dad swore that we had already passed Punkin Center and just hadn't noticed it in dark. The idea wasn't that far-fetched since there were no roadside lights and I could easily believe that, if the town wasn't smack dab in the middle of the road, we could have driven by it without noticing.

This not so amusing game went on for a while. Dad kept saying, "Oh, we're good for another 20 miles," then we'd drive another 20 miles. He'd repeat, with fading confidence, "I'm certain we're good for another 20 miles." I'm no math wizard and wasn't very worldly at the ripe old age of twelve, but I can tell you the numbers didn't add up. He had been repeating this mantra for at least 45 minutes, and I started to feel a little insecure. Not only were there no services or streetlights, but there was also a noticeable lack of traffic on this stretch of road that did not appear on any printed map in the known universe. I started to imagine in my mind one of those animal skulls that you see out in the desert just lying there, cracked and dried by the side of the road. Sometimes, those skulls looked disconcertingly human.

Abruptly, Dad shouted, "There's a town! Look!" Wide-eyed and anxious, we all stared out the windshield. Sure enough, we approached an intersection and a sign that read "Punkin Center." In the feverish dreams brought on by extreme hunger, I had formed a clear image in my mind of what a town called Punkin Center would look like: I imagined the center of a bustling little western town, with a main street café and people strolling about and talking to one another on street corners. They would welcome forlorn out-of-towners with open arms and bacon sandwiches. Unfortunately, I was wrong. Dead wrong. Punkin Center consisted of the following: one trailer and one gas pump. That was it. One lonely trailer and a solitary gas pump. No bustling townsfolk, no busy city center, and, most importantly, *no bacon sandwiches*. I knew at that point the advanced stages of starvation had set in. I was finally having hallucinations and everything, because the sign said "Center," and there sat only one trailer and a gas pump! Yeah, it was the center all right: the dead-end center of nowhere. Dad, on the other hand, grinned from ear to ear, convinced by that time that we would certainly run out of gas, and given the amount of traffic on the road I am not sure those animal skulls rotting out there in the desert didn't enter his mind. The one thing in the world that Dad wanted at that moment was a gas pump. So Punkin Center looked pretty appealing to him, notwithstanding the clear lack of civilization.

Dad beamed ecstatically when he pulled up next to the pump, though there appeared to be no one around. Dad honked the horn and a few minutes later a gentleman came out of the trailer. All I could think of when I saw him was, "Please don't say anything about another *short cut*!" Dad told the guy that he desperately needed some gasoline. The guy told Dad that he couldn't sell him any gas because the pump belonged to the state. Dad responded that he couldn't care less who owned the damned pump, but that we couldn't drive another mile without some gas. He also added that our family, who happened to be starving at the time, would happily join the gentleman in his trailer for a nice, hot dinner and then a night of respite—free of charge, of course—before Dad could set out on his own for gas the next morning. At the time, I didn't understand the effectiveness of this negotiation tactic, but it took the gentleman about two seconds to change his mind about selling Dad some fuel. Dad thanked him for his help and we headed back down Prairie Road towards Colorado Springs.

About ten minutes later we arrived in Rush, an actual town with actual people and actual restaurants. It appeared the hand-drawn map wasn't to scale. We got something to eat and drove until we arrived at Mom and Dad's friends' house in the wee hours of the morning. As soon as we arose the next morning, my Mom's friend led us outside to see Pikes Peak. Fresh snow covered the Rockies and the sky looked crystal blue; it was a cold, clear morning and it seemed you could see for miles. The memory still brings tears to my eyes. It was one of the most beautiful sights I had ever seen, even to this day.

That ominous, purple, sleeping giant from the night before turned out to be extraordinarily beautiful, a jagged expression of geological power that, ironically, radiated peace and assurance. Although we lived in Colorado Springs for three years, I gazed at Pikes Peak every day with just as much admiration and wonder as I had that very first morning . . . except, of course, in the summertime, when it just looked like a big ol' pile of dirt.

****

One last piece of information concerning Prairie Road seems in order. A few years later, my Uncle Irvin and Aunt Helen decided to visit us in Colorado. Of course, Dad had to call up and tell Uncle Irvin about the short cut to Colorado Springs by way of Prairie Road. I remember the last thing he said to Irvin was to be sure and fill up in Sharon Springs. I have always heard that guys have a problem *asking* for directions, but experience tells me they clearly have a problem *following* directions. Uncle Irvin decided that the car had plenty of gas when they arrived in Sharon Springs, and therefore, he didn't stop to fill up the tank. Uncle Irvin drove a Mercury Marquis, which I am not aware was ever classified as an economy car, as far as gas mileage goes. Nonetheless, he convinced himself that he didn't need to fill the tank in Sharon Springs. They didn't even make it to Punkin Center before they ran out of gas. I can only imagine what Aunt Helen—who has an annoyingly high-pitched, squeaky voice— sounded like during the two-hour lecture of everything that Irvin has done wrong in his life up to that point in time.

When they finally arrived at our home, Mom and Aunt Helen, ever sisters, re-bonded instantaneously. The first thing out of Aunt Helen's mouth was the story of how Irvin didn't stop and get gas and how long they sat stranded in the center of nowhere. But Irwin and Dad seemed to take it in stride, expecting the expected, so they shuffled off to the den to watch a random sporting event while the women sat at the kitchen table exchanging stories of male stubbornness and irresponsibility.

I think that somehow they found comfort in knowing that there was absolutely nothing they could have done to make the situation any better, since it is so deeply embedded in the genetic code of men that they must take magical *short cuts* and refuse to follow anyone else's directions. Both Mom and Aunt Helen had several stories supporting this biological theory, and as one would finish, the other would try to top it. It's funny how men seem to bond by taking comfort in knowing that the mistakes that they made are mere repetitions of the mistakes of their ancestors and how women seem to bond by telling as many other women as they can about all those same mistakes unswervingly committed by the men in their lives.

Home Sick

After leaving the comforts of Indiana and with the holiday season approaching, Mom and Dad knew that if we didn't go home for Christmas, the family would never forgive us. We had never spent the holidays separated from the family; so clearly, a mere phone call would not suffice. We planned to drive home a few days before Christmas and stay for a week.

Anticipation for the holiday season filled Tara and me. A week crawled by at the pace of a year as Christmas approached. Occupying my spare time became my only method of retaining my sanity, and besides, I enjoyed doing crafts. It didn't matter what kind of crafts; I loved making something out of nothing. One day in early December that year, I surveyed the *Good Housekeeping* and *Family Circle* magazines as we stood in the checkout lane in the grocery store. I saw the most beautiful gingerbread church on the cover of one of the magazines, and I became immediately intrigued by it. I asked Mom if she would buy the magazine so that I could get the pattern and make the gingerbread ensemble. I knew it was a significant request, as Mom carefully watched every penny she spent. Her frugality wasn't driven by selfishness, but instead by her past, years of stretching the few remaining dollars for a week's worth of groceries after paying all the essential obligations, such as rent, utilities and gas to get to work. Money in the bank represented financial security for the family and Mom saved every cent she could to build on that security. Regardless, on that cold, December day, her instincts told her that my heart pined to build that church and that my sanity—and perhaps hers, as she must've realized—depended on it. I never asked for much, and that day I felt elated when Mom agreed to buy the magazine for me.

I cut out the patterns, Mom purchased all the necessary ingredients that I needed, and about a week before we departed for Indiana, I constructed the gingerbread church. The task proved to be a bit more difficult than I originally thought. A steeple with a bell tower on it topped the church, which was tricky enough to construct. In addition, the project encompassed more than just a church, but an entire bucolic scene complete with a horse drawn carriage, a snowy expanse of lawn, and several pine trees. Still, I found the intricacy of the gingerbread concoction appealing. After rolling out the dough and carving out the individual pieces, we baked the gingerbread and prepared to assemble the church and its environs.

The pieces didn't fit together as nicely as I had hoped, but the instructions read to fill the gaps with a powdered sugar icing that we made to stick the pieces together, the result being that the scene appeared a bit snowier than the original magazine illustration. I doggedly worked on the gingerbread church, along with all the other pieces of the scene, most of the day one Sunday. After I completed it, the scene looked almost as beautiful as the picture. I felt happy that we had a week to enjoy it before we left for Indiana.

The next weekend while we packed the trunk of the car in preparation for our trip, Mom asked me if I wanted to take my gingerbread church to Indiana. She knew how proud I was of it and thought it would be nice if everyone back home could enjoy it. Although thrilled, I couldn't imagine how to successfully transport the ensemble. Mom found a box that fit behind the driver's seat on the floor, and we placed the church and the rest of the pieces in the box for safekeeping. The box didn't have a lid, as the frosting needed to remain dry in order for the pieces to stay adhered to one another. Having the box right at my feet was uncomfortable, because then I had nowhere to put them, but ultimately, I didn't mind. I was just glad that we took my creation with us. The box was primarily on my side of the car, though Tara's side was partially obstructed as well, although she didn't complain either, as her anticipation of starting our latest expedition over road any self-serving concerns of confinement.

We drove non-stop, except for the occasional filling station interruption—no spending the night at some motel like other sissy families might. I think this tendency arises from the same male gene that prevents men from asking for directions, but Dad wanted to get to Indiana in the least amount of time. And, of course, Mom had the frugality gene living inside her, so she didn't complain about the long drive and lack of sleep, since it saved us money by driving through the night. The only potential obstacle to slow us down was the weather: as only a few days remained before Christmas, and we travelled across the northern part of the United States. Naturally, snow fell from the sky unabated. Dad had a lot of experience driving in the snow, however, so we didn't think much of it. But the farther we drove, the heavier the snow fell. Dad seemed unconcerned, which reassured us, and besides, we knew he wasn't about to stop and let the storm pass.

When we traveled long distances in the car, we passed time by singing songs. We knew all different kinds of songs. On this particular night, we sang a song that went something like, "Oh mama, who's that looking in my window?" I don't remember the rest of the words, but we tooled down the highway in a blizzard singing this song. Suddenly, the cars in front of us started fishtailing. Cars slid off the road, onto the shoulder and the median. Some cars veered left and some cars skidded right, and some of the vehicles spun in circles. It appeared that all the cars but ours had lost control. We sang, "Oh mama," as we watched the intricate ballet of spinning, lurching cars, and then everyone fell silent, holding our breaths, awaiting the eminent crash. But Dad drove right through the middle of the cars and out of danger, and he turned back to us and said, "Why'd everyone stop singing?" We all breathed a sigh of relief and started singing once more, "Oh mama, who's that looking in my window?"

Abruptly, Tara cried, "OH MAMA!" as if something terrible had occurred. I looked over at her and saw that she had her foot planted firmly inside the box that held my gingerbread church. I guess in all the excitement, she had inadvertently put her foot down in the box and didn't even notice. My stomach sank. I didn't want to look in the box, but I had to know. I peaked gingerly over the top of the half-buckled box and into the shards of gingerbread that were strewn, willy-nilly, over the bottom. Unfortunately, my gingerbread church didn't resemble a church anymore, but instead, a landscape reminiscent of the aftermath of a direct hit from an F4 tornado. One of the horses, that before appeared to energetically pull the sled passing in front of the church, lay on its side, impaled by the sharp point of the steeple that once rose proudly above the roof of the church. I became instantly devastated. All my hard work (you would have thought that it took me a year to build it) was gone in an instant. All that remained were broken pieces of gingerbread covered with powdered sugar frosting. Even Tara's foot was covered with frosting, and we grabbed whatever rags we could find in the car and cleaned up the mess.

The next time that we stopped for gas, Mom removed the box from the car and took it inside the gas station. She walked up to the counter with the box and asked the attendant if she could dump the box anywhere. The attendant, an old, Colorado mountain man, looked at her with a puzzled expression on his face and said, "Can ya eat it?" Mom said of course you could and explained that it was gingerbread. But before Mom could inform the gentleman that her daughter had inadvertently put her foot through it, he picked up a piece of it, stuck it in his mouth and started chewing on it. He said it tasted downright delicious! He asked if he could keep the whole box and before Mom could say anything, he quickly stashed it behind the counter. That made the whole incident nearly worthwhile for me since my first attempt at cooking gingerbread ended on a high note. Not only had I created a beautiful church scene, at least while it lasted, but it also tasted good. Although we didn't have the gingerbread church to show everyone back home, we had pictures of it and a great story to tell.

****

We had a wonderful time back home in Indiana for the holidays. Everyone acted fairly impressed when they saw the pictures of my gingerbread church and thought the story of its demise was sad, but appropriately amusing, since they all were well aware that something always went askew when our family traveled. Of course, the icing on the cake (or gingerbread in this case) was ending the story with the rugged mountain man that ate the confection after Tara had put her foot in it.

Christmas was always eventful at Grandma Grace's house, foot-flavored gingerbread aside. Both of Dad's siblings, Uncle Wayne, Aunt Joyce and her family participated in the festivities. Joy was our considerably younger cousin, probably four or five years old at that time and possessed a real prissy personality. Mom crocheted her a skirt for Christmas and back then we never thought of buying gift boxes to put things in before wrapping them. Our family saved empty boxes for the sole purpose of wrapping presents that needed a container around them. For Joy's skirt, the box of choice that year was a Zesta cracker box. Joy rapidly ripped pieces of paper off the gift and when she completely removed the last of the wrapping paper, she started crying. We asked her what was wrong and she said, "Crackers, and I don't even like that kind!" All the adults tried repeatedly to get her to open the cracker box so that she would discover her skirt. She was not the least bit interested in opening the box. After enough prodding, she finally relented and discovered the skirt. Her frown quickly turned into a smile when she realized that she didn't have a box of crackers, but a pretty skirt to wear. Most children are not that pleased to receive clothing, but compared to a box of saltine crackers, she thought it was a nifty gift.

Joy's initial disappointment with her present didn't quite hold a candle to Grandma Grace's that year. Grace turned her natural talent for snooping into an undeniable art form around the holidays, because she just had to know ahead of time what she was getting for Christmas. Every year, the task for the entire family was to surprise Grace with a gift that she didn't expect and couldn't guess the contents. That particular year, my Uncle Wayne had bought her a silver tea serving set. He found a huge box to put it in, but realized that, if Grace figured out that the box felt too light, she would know that the box wasn't full, but instead being used as a decoy from its true contents. Determined to disguise the silver tea set, Uncle Wayne procured an old washing machine motor and put it in the bottom of the box. The motor made the box very heavy, and Wayne felt confident that she wouldn't be able to figure out that the box actually contained her real present, the silver tea service.

When the time came to open presents, Grandma Grace acted more than anxious to open the box from Wayne. She had stewed all week about it, perplexed that she couldn't generate a single guess as to what the box contained. She tore into the wrapping paper and yanked open the box. Another, much smaller box lay inside, which contained her silver tea service, but she shoved it aside and started rummaging through the newspapers in an attempt to reach the bottom of the box. When she finally discovered the motor, she lifted it up to show everyone. It was heavy, filthy, and covered with grease. With a puzzled look on her face, she turned to Wayne and said, "Well, I think it's a motor, but what am I supposed to do with it?" We all got a good laugh out of the whole incident, watching Grandma Grace—usually so clever—rummage around the silver tea service amid all the newspapers in the box only to discover a nasty old motor. Of course, she felt thrilled after discovering that the motor posed a mere distraction and did not represent her intended gift.

Grandma Grace received a lot of pleasure from teasing Tara and me. She was a gray-haired ball of energy and always up to mischief. As we grew up, Grandma Grace derived great pleasure from telling Tara and me that we were going to get a bundle of switches from Santa Claus if we weren't good. Tara and I behaved especially well in the month of December, thinking that maybe we had some things to make up for and hoping that the most current events would outweigh past sins. Our thinking followed the reasoning that maybe we could skate by and escape punishment for some of the less complimentary deeds we had done throughout the year. We had always, as of yet, avoided the bundle of switches from Santa. But, as we grew older, we finally realized that it was an idle threat, an attempt to trick us into behaving. The particular year we fully realized this little deceit, we decided to have some fun with Grandma Grace, though I have to admit thoughts of revenge lurked in our minds as well.

Grandma Grace always stayed up really late, waiting to make sure that we had finished our bathroom duties for the night, and then she retired to the bathroom for the last few hours of the evening. She kept crossword puzzles in the bathroom that she worked on into the wee hours of the morning. I considered it strange at the time and couldn't figure out why she waited to go to the bathroom until everyone else was finished. Truth be told, she had trouble pooping. She sat for hours, attempting to will her bowels into movement. Sometimes she succeeded (mind over matter, oh that's gross), but the nights she didn't, the next morning her enema bag laid draining in the sink. TMI? Regardless, the bottom line is that Grace was always the last one in the house to crawl into bed. This fact made the plan that Tara and I had devised rather more difficult, but certainly not impossible—not for two kids hell-bent on exacting a little payback from their feisty Grandma.

Tara and I had spent the day secretly collecting some fine tree branches from the front yard. We tied them into a bundle with a red ribbon and placed a gift tag on them that read "To: Grace, From: Santa." We hid them out of sight but practically died with the anticipation of placing them under the tree after everyone had retired for the evening, so that in the morning, they would be lying there for everyone to see. It seemed like an eternity, but when Grace finally went to bed, we placed the switches front and center beneath the Christmas tree. The next morning when Grandma Grace began passing out the gifts, we all knew the exact moment when she realized the switches were addressed to her. The squeal that escaped her mouth that morning assured me that she was truly surprised. She acted thrilled at being singled out, knowing full well that the switches weren't from Old Saint Nick, but instead, a family member who wished to play a gag on her. Although her shear existence longed to pull the perfect prank, she was titillated by the seamless execution of the event that day. She insisted on having her picture taken with the branches and the ear-to-ear grin on her face showed her love of practical jokes. Needless to say, Tara and I never admitted that we were the ones who perpetrated the prank, but I'm pretty sure that Grandma Grace figured it out. After that Christmas, she never threatened us with a bundle of switches again. In order to preserve the memory, Tara and I made sure that our younger cousins knew the whole story so Grandma Grace would think twice about using the threat of receiving switches from Santa on them.

To this day, everyone in our family can truthfully state that Grace is the only one in our family who ever actually received a bundle of switches from Santa. Although if I wasn't here to tell you the story and confirm that I witnessed the ordeal, I don't think you would ever get her to admit it freely. That was my last Christmas in Indiana as a child, albeit one of the most memorable. The presents under the Christmas tree that year reminded me a lot like that MasterCard commercial: Dad's new sweater, $20; Sheryl's new doll, $30; Tara's new winter coat, $40.   Seeing Grandma Grace's face when she realized that the switches were addressed to her: Priceless!

52 Pick Up

While Tara and I grew up, our parents eagerly played card games every chance they had. We spent many hours in the evenings and on the weekends playing games with the family. Most people choose the size of their family by considering how much time they can spend with their children and how financially sound they are. Contrarily, when you come from a card-playing family, these logical considerations have no bearing on family size. The number of children that avid card players rear is based on how many additional people they require for a good game of cards. Mom and Dad usually played card games in which two people partner against two other people. The fact that I have one sibling is strictly based on the fact that Mom and Dad needed two other people to partner with. Four people form the perfect card-playing unit, and, as such, they decided instantly that two children made the perfect family size. Being the younger of the two, I feel thankful that it doesn't just take three people for the perfect game, or I might not exist today.

The competitive nature of my parents and cards started when, as young adults, they played cards with my grandparents, who kept a minimum of twenty decks of cards in their house. They participated in a wide variety of games and had many specialized decks that suited each game, such as Euchre, Rook, and Pinochle. They also had regular decks of 52 cards that sufficed for games such as Hearts and Spades. They didn't just own one deck of each kind, though, because they considered decks of cards like money in the bank. They could never have too much, or too many. As the cards became worn and they bought new decks, the old decks remained in the drawer. Even with bent corners and with the lamination separating, they kept the decks for a rainy day, just in case for some reason, the world suddenly became void of cards.

I watched them play for hours, and learned a lot from sitting beside one of them while studying their strategy as they played the game. Invariably, the men partnered and played against the women. It seemed that sometimes one team won most of the games, and other nights the other team won the majority. I noticed throughout my life that many people become discouraged if they lose repeatedly and choose to quit, hoping that next time their luck improves. But that behavior was foreign to this group. My family hates to quit when they fall behind, because the winning team will tease them unmercifully until the next time they play cards. The farther behind one team got, the more determined that team became. As for the winning team, they could just forget about quitting, because the losing team would hold them hostage at the card table all night in an attempt to catch up.

One particular Friday night, we went to the grandparent's house for a visit. The four adults sat down at the kitchen table and commenced to playing cards. The women experienced a tough battle of it that night, as luck was not on their side. I can't remember who started it, but either Mom or Grandma Grace became highly frustrated, grabbed the deck of cards and started ripping it up. Determined to change their luck, she knew that many decks—perhaps luckier decks—waited in the drawer for their turn on the kitchen table. I can't even remember what game they played that evening, but as the night wore on, the women continued to lose. They had clearly reached their breaking point as the evening wore on, and every time they lost another game, they destroyed another deck of cards. Eventually, they had shredded every deck for each particular game they played, which forced them to switch to a different game, and the cycle would begin all over. Alas, it didn't matter what game they played, the women just couldn't win a game of cards that night.

Tara and I woke up the next morning on the floor with a couple of rugs over the top of us and the sound of ripping cards filling our ears. The fatigued adults sat at the kitchen table. The scowls on the women's faces indicated to me that they had not lost their will to prevail. I guess since the game never ended, Tara and I fell asleep on the kitchen floor. Apparently, the women didn't want to waste any time putting us to bed, so Grandma Grace just took a couple rugs and covered us up.

I looked around, a bit disoriented when I saw the pile of shredded playing cards lying there beside the table. I found the series of events intriguing. It reminded me of one of those celebrations where people smash perfectly good plates on the floor or throw wine glasses into the fireplace. I wondered if they had started a new tradition that evening, secretly hoping they had. By the end of the following afternoon, every deck of cards at my grandparents' house had been destroyed. I kept my distance from that point on, since the women's frames of mind appeared less than stable. When I heard my Grandma Grace say they had emptied all the decks from the card drawer, I thought thank goodness; despite my earlier enthusiasm for this strange, new tradition, I realized by then that something unpleasant would happen if the adults continued their marathon. I presume that 99 percent of people at that point would admit defeat and lick their wounds. As well, these adults clearly suffered from a lack of sleep and food over an incredible amount of time. But, instead of behaving like rational people and ending the torment, they just went to the store and got more cards! I think everyone would agree that my family has an obsession when it comes to card games—an obsession that could be more accurately described as a form of mental illness.

I have no idea of the final outcome that day, as I decided to make myself scarce until the dust settled. Truthfully, I don't think such a situation could ever be fully resolved in my family. The adults still talk about that night, as if it were a game-changing historical event in the life of our family. Before my Grandpa Willard died, he'd sit at the kitchen table and tell stories about the significant events in his life. He spoke of the time that he broke his arm starting one of the old crank-start cars. He reminisced about the time when the farm burned down and his friend Bill died. And, oh yeah, let's not forget about the time when *Mom and Grandma Grace tore up every deck of cards in the house while trying desperately to change their luck.*

Tara and I spent many hours at the card table with Mom and Dad. Dad and I always partnered, as did Tara and Mom. By now you probably noticed that Mom and Dad never played partners together, and this probably explains how they stayed married for over 55 years. In all card games, a strategy exists for getting the most points, (or the least points in the game of Hearts), towards winning the game. In the game of Rook, for example, the person who bids the highest chooses the trump suit and must catch the number of points, or higher, than they bid. For instance, if you bid 100 points, you and your partner must catch 100 points or more, otherwise your tally towards the game is decreased by whatever you bid. In this case, your team's score would be reduced by 100 points. Also in the game of Rook, not all the cards represent points, so the object of the game is to catch the most cards that count. This is called *catching game.* Dad's mantra was, "Always play your partner for game." This phrase meant that if you place your card on the table before your partner's turn and the highest card that can catch the trick (the cards on the table) has not yet been played, you are supposed to play a game card (one that counts towards points) and hope your partner catches it. Not only are you tasked with remembering all the strategies of the game, you must remember every card that was previously played so that you know what cards are still in the players' hands. This isn't easy for adults, let alone children, but it's a necessary skill for effective card competition.

One evening we sat down to play Rook and, as usual, Dad and I partnered against Tara and Mom. Dad and I kept losing and fell a couple of games behind our opponents. Of course, Mom and Tara couldn't resist rubbing salt in our wounds. Dad became increasingly irritated as we played. The next thing I knew, I missed a play and Dad stood up and yelled, "I told you to ALWAYS PLAY YOUR PARTNER FOR GAME!!" I knew that I had messed up so I leaned forward, put my head on the table and pretended to cry. I knew that Dad couldn't stand it when I cried. He banged his fist on the table and shouted, "IT'S ONLY A GAME!" When he suddenly realized what he had said while pounding his fist and shouting, a pitiful look appeared on his face and we all busted out laughing.

Chalk it up to another historical event in the life of my family: we will never let Dad forget that outburst. I know that when I grow old and sit at the kitchen table telling significant stories about my life, I will tell the tale of Dad's insistence that playing cards was ONLY A GAME! After all, winning and losing at cards might as well be a life and death situation in my family. The sheer torture of losing and having to hear about it for days or weeks is truly a fate worse than death. Thank goodness we all believe in the afterlife.

God's Gentle Creatures

Once again my nomadic father decided that the time had come for us to become acquainted with a new state and we relocated to Ogden, Utah. When we lived on the farm, we could have all the animals we wanted. After we relocated to town, the only animals Mom permitted in the house had to live in a cage or a bowl and be smaller than an average-size tomato. That rule limited us to fish, small lizards, and hamsters. Despite such limitations, Tara and I never lost our adoration for animals. One of my most unusual pets that fit into Mom's well-defined, although strictly confined guidelines was a hybrid freshwater fish that I named Buggy. Shiny, black scales covered his body, and he had a feathery tail that split into three triangular-shaped pieces. His enormous eyes protruded unblinkingly, grotesquely out of each side of his head—hence, the name Buggy. When I saw him in the store, I felt sorry for him because I thought he was deformed. My love for him grew through time but, as a busy and easily distracted teenager, I didn't always set aside time to clean his bowl regularly.

My Mom, on the other hand, insisted upon everything being clean and in its designated place. Once a week we vacuumed, dusted, changed the linens and scrubbed the bathrooms. Our weekly ritual ensured that everything stayed spotless. Some weekends my schedule was just too full to squeeze in cleaning Buggy's bowl. After a particularly hectic weekend, Mom took pity on me and decided she would help me finish my chores by cleaning Buggy's bowl. This chore consisted of transferring Buggy into a bucket full of fresh water, so you could clean the sides of his regular bowl, then flush out the rocks in the bottom with fresh water until no debris floated around in the water. Then you refilled the bowl with fresh water and transferred

Buggy back into his freshly cleaned home. Buggy loved fresh water and Mom liked everything sparkling clean, so everyone would be happy. Seems simple, doesn't it?

As I studied in my room that day, suddenly I heard Mom yell, "Oh no! Sheryl, come in here. Your fish is dead!" I ran into the kitchen and looked in the bucket. Buggy's black scales had turned white around the edges and he floated upside down in the bucket. I sadly scooped him up in my hand and, as I touched the water where he floated motionless, I jerked my hand back instinctively: the water was hot! Not scalding, perhaps, but very, very warm. Mom, possessing the clean gene, was so used to putting hot water in the bucket that, without thinking, she had filled the bucket with hot water instead of cold. She felt horrible about taking Buggy's life, but that wasn't the first time Mom or Dad had accidentally killed a pet. Though upset, I had grown accustomed to the unfortunate reality that my pets may, and probably would, experience death-defying peril under my watch.

After Buggy's demise, I decided that I wanted a pet that I could play with. Fish are pretty to look at (at least some fish are), but you can't handle them. When I started musing over what kind of pet I could get that was smaller than a tomato but that I could hold, I immediately thought of a lizard that Tara and I had played with back on the farm. That led me to purchase Newton. Newton was a newt, or a black salamander. When I bought him, the guy in the pet store told me that he ate mealworms for nutrition. The mealworms came dried in a box, all compressed together, so the guy showed me how to break off a small chunk and put it in some water. As the dried mass slowly absorbed the moisture, the mealworms softened and expanded so the newt could eat them. After I took Newton home, I broke off a small portion of mealworms and placed it in the water for Newton every day when I got home from school. After a week or so, the water in his bowl appeared murky and I noticed that a bunch of mealworms still floated in the water. I assumed that I was over-feeding Newton, so after cleaning his bowl I fed him a little less each time. But this didn't seem to alleviate the situation and his water continued to look foggy. Still, I continued to put a fresh portion of mealworms in his bowl each day, since I had never had a live-in lizard before and wasn't really sure how much they should eat.

One day when I got home from school, I went to feed Newton and became startled when I noticed that his left foot was gone. All that was left was a tiny stub that protruded from his body where his foot used to be. He still walked around with ease, it seemed, but he had no left foot. After thinking about it for a while, I remembered hearing that some animals would consume their own limbs if they were starving. Well, I thought, the only way Newton could be starving is if he couldn't find his food. So I took some mealworms, soaked them in the water and put them on the end of my index finger. I gently touched the tip of his mouth with them and he immediately lunged forward towards my finger with his mouth wide open. His sandpaper teeth stuck in my flesh and his mouth jammed, fully opened around my finger. I moved my finger back a bit and he instantly gobbled up the mealworms. I repeated this about four or five times before he acted satisfied. It was at that point that I realized why his food never disappeared. I concluded that he was either blind or couldn't smell, regardless, he couldn't find his dinner.

From that day forward, every day when I returned home from school, I hand-fed Newton, or should I more accurately say, finger-fed him. He lived for about a year, and never seemed to be bothered by the fact that he had a missing foot. I think I felt more upset about it than he did. But mealtime became our quality time together, each day when I would place the mealworms on the end of my finger. He crawled up and feasted until his belly felt full.

* * * * * * * * * * * * * * * * * * *

Pets that live in bowls are better than nothing, but I really wanted a pet that had fur, something that I could cuddle with. Therefore, I graduated from pets that lived in bowls to pets that lived in cages. I never forgot the hamster that I had at the house on Mary Ann Drive and I really enjoyed him. So, I bought another hamster, a golden one this time, and named him Dirtbag. I took him out of his cage and played with him on my bed. He was very good-natured. We even had snacks together. His favorite snack was peanut butter. I would put a dab on my finger at night before I went to bed, and Dirtbag would eagerly lick my finger clean. Peanut butter coated his two front teeth while he ate. As soon as he finished eating, he would clean himself thoroughly and thus smell like a jar of peanut butter for the rest of the evening. Sometimes after his post-snack cleaning, he would still have peanut butter stuck between his two front chompers, but that was easily remedied with one quick swipe of dental floss. Dirtbag was a good sport about it and I believed he shared my desire for him to follow good dental hygiene. That became our nightly tradition.

He lived in an extensive Habitrail cage, but he became bored from being boxed in, and repeatedly shoved and pushed on the doors, trying to escape. He eventually broke off one of the plastic tabs that locked one of the doors in place, but never successfully got it open—at least not until I decided to visit a friend in another state for a week. I didn't stop to consider what would happen if Dirtbag didn't receive his evening snack of peanut butter. I think the lack of attention (and daily ration of peanut butter) that week made him dead serious about breaking out in the middle of the night. I guess he figured if no one brought him his snack, he would go and get it himself.

One night while I vacationed in Colorado and Mom and Dad slept peacefully in their bed, something decided to crawl up Dad's leg. Instinctively, Dad hit it before he realized what, or should I say who, it was. "Oh Linda!" He yelled, startling my sleeping Mom. "Get up.

I think I just killed Dirtbag!" They threw the covers back and saw Dirtbag crouched in the middle of the bed, dazed and spinning in circles. He acted completely befuddled. Whenever he tried to move, he just spun sadly in one direction. Mom reached down gently to pick him up and said, "Oh, come here Dirtbag." The hamster shot straight up in the air at her touch, just like he was attached to a spring. He landed in the covers on the floor and the chase ensued. He took off like his life depended on it, and I'm pretty sure he thought it did. Poor thing: he was probably thinking that all he wanted was a little peanut butter and now some giant was trying to kill him. The cruelty of life!

Mom and Dad finally captured him from behind the refrigerator and returned him to his cage. When I got home and they told me the story, I couldn't believe that he had actually escaped. From that day forward, if I was gone, even for one night, Mom and Dad made sure that Dirtbag got his peanut butter before bedtime, and we never had another jail break.

****

As time passed, I really thought that Dirtbag needed some companionship—that is, besides me. I thought another hamster would make a good friend for him. So, I went to the pet store and bought a white, teddy bear hamster and named him Mr. Clean. It didn't really work out very well, because Mr. Clean didn't take a liking to Dirtbag, and vice versa; perhaps my choice of names was sadly prophetic. They never did become attached to one another, and usually stayed on opposite sides of the Habitrail. Thank goodness it was big enough for them both to have their own space.

Mr. Clean enjoyed the exercise ball that I had originally bought for Dirtbag. The ball was constructed of clear plastic with holes in it for ventilation; the top screwed off of it and you put a hamster inside it. Then when you sat it down on the floor, the hamster ran all over the house in the bubble. He wouldn't get loose or stepped on. I used to place Mr. Clean in the ball when Mom and/or Dad and I watched TV in the evening. Usually we got more enjoyment out of Mr. Clean's ball maneuvers than the TV program we watched. He rolled through the living room, frequently stopping in front of the TV as if he wanted to make sure we noticed him. He took off on the carpeted floor, accelerating through the dining room, passing under the table through the maze of chair legs, and hit the tiled floor of the kitchen at full speed, gliding across the waxed floor and crashing into the refrigerator. He'd shake his head, turn around and roll back into the living room, stopping to clean himself as we complimented him on his daring feat of precision. He seemed to enjoy it best when we'd honor him with a round of applause. He had hours of fun with that, and we had a lot of enjoyment watching him.

Eventually, my hamsters passed on from old age. The timing was right, though, because I had become engaged and was preparing to get married. The time had arrived for me to leave the nest and build my own home. I looked forward to my new life. No more rules to follow; no more permission to ask—but then again, this also meant there was no one to pay my rent or tuition.

Once I left home, I quickly realized that life without rules introduced chaos. Tara and I had the recipe for a structured life passed down to us from Mom. However, the method in which we mixed all the ingredients changed the final product. Just like a delicate soufflé, even when everything looks perfect, it can collapse at the last minute. No amount of preparation and care can always prevent havoc. Tara knows it and I know it, primarily from first-hand experience.

Houston, We Have a Problem

Utah's beauty rivaled that of Colorado, with the only familiar sight being the majestic Rocky Mountains. Tara, true to form, remained completely distraught and devastated by the move. She was a senior in high school and very active in her old school in Colorado. In addition, she missed her boyfriend, Jerry, terribly. They talked on the phone daily, but their frequent conversations didn't fulfill her needs for his companionship. As a typical 17 year old girl (Jerry was eight years her senior), she was in love with the idea of being in love, and she was head over heels for Jerry. It didn't hurt that he was older and therefore infinitely more sophisticated and independent than Tara could ever be—at least so she thought at the time. Tara planned to graduate from high school after the winter semester when we lived in Colorado. But Utah didn't have the early graduation option and as such, required her to attend the entire year of her senior class. That didn't make her very happy either.

Jerry's term in the army ended shortly after we moved, so he entered the real world as a civilian and headed to Utah to be with Tara. The two of them had decided to get married, which Mom and Dad accepted, albeit not happily. This struck me as a bit of hypocrisy, though: after all, when Mom and Dad eloped, she was only 17, so history was merely repeating itself. Mom and Dad had lived through the same scenario and knew that if they didn't give their consent, chances were that Tara and Jerry would just take off anyway, as Mom and Dad had years before, leaving Mom to this day with no high school diploma. Thus, they relented and give their somewhat reluctant blessing. Tara and Jerry decided to go to Elko, Nevada to get married since there was no waiting period between the time a couple purchased a marriage license and the moment they said their vows—contrary to the laws in the state of Utah at the time (and most states still. Nevada remains the capital of the quick wedding).

On the pre-selected day of the nuptials, Mom, Dad and I headed west in the Mercury Marquis that they owned, followed by Tara and Jerry in his Pontiac Firebird. About four hours later, we arrived in Elko, where we went straight to the courthouse. Tara and Jerry purchased a license and were immediately thereafter married by the Justice of the Peace. Jerry wore a white dress shirt with a dark brown tie and beige-colored, bell-bottomed slacks. Tara wore an unadorned white dress that hit her mid-thigh. She looked beautiful with her long, thick, shiny black hair, donning a simple, short veil. The five-minute ceremony occurred uneventfully—to the point of being boring— although the excitement that Tara clearly felt emanated from her to me, which gave me butterflies in anticipation of her new life that was about to begin.

Before we had left Utah, finally gripped by the happiness of an impending union, Mom had prepared small bags of birdseed that we could toss as Tara and Jerry exited the courthouse. As the Justice of the Peace announced them husband and wife, Mom, Dad and I quickly left the small room in which the ceremony was held, attempting to get out in front of the newlyweds and surprise them with a shower of birdseed, wishing them eternal happiness.

As we scurried down the courthouse steps, searching for the perfect position, I noticed an unnatural number of birds hanging around. They didn't seem a bit concerned by our presence, but instead walked around us as if we were members of their clan. I didn't have much time to ponder the implications of such a fine-feathered gathering, as Tara and Jerry suddenly opened the door and walked out to the edge of the top step; the three of us began deluging them with a birdseed shower. Almost immediately, the birds took to low-orbit flight, hundreds of them it seemed, frantically snatching the seeds in a flurry of activity. They started landing on top of Tara's head, and she began waving her arms and ducking down in order to ward off her attackers, but the birds continued to flock to her. Apparently, the small veil that sat atop her head was bunched up just below the headpiece, and the gathered tulle had created small crevices just the right size in which to collect maximum birdseed. The frenzied birds continued to peck at the top of the veil, trying to collect the tiny morsels. Tara continued to wave her arms, screaming, "Get them off of me!" The scene resembled something out of the movie *The Birds,* with Tara substituting for Tippi Hedren, but believe me, Tara wasn't acting. Desperate to relieve Tara's terror, Jerry reached out and snatched the veil off the top of her head. The swift, full-armed movement caused Jerry to lose his balance, and as he tried to recover, his legs frantically tried to right him although they couldn't get traction. The steps, covered in birdseed, had become a safety hazard for the newlyweds, and Jerry quickly ended up on his butt, two steps from the top. Perhaps we should have known that the full-out attack of the birds on Tara and Jerry's wedding day represented an omen of things to come, but as our family revels in the bizarre happenstance, we all just laughed about it as we enjoyed one of our last meals together as one rather small but certainly happy family.

Tara and Jerry lived in Ogden for three more months, contented in their early marital bliss, although Jerry struggled to find full-time employment. After Tara completed her fall semester, she and Jerry returned to Colorado where she received her diploma for high school. Since Jerry hadn't been successful at securing a job that would support his new family, he re-enlisted in the army and they relocated to the state of Washington. It definitely wasn't his first choice for employment, but he knew the army offered stable income and steady work. As well, to Jerry's chagrin, the mess hall offered up tastier meals than Tara's attempts in their kitchen at home.

After Tara left, I continued through high school without my constant companion (though with a bevy of new animal friends as recounted above). I had just gotten my driver's license, which proved challenging since my sense of direction had been upset by the move. In Colorado, I used the mountains as my compass. It didn't matter whether you were inside the city or outside, because the sight of the towering mountains on the western horizon always reminded you in what direction you were heading. When we moved to Utah, we lived on the opposite side of the Rockies, so the mountains rose up on the eastern horizon. Invariably, when my instinct told me to turn right, in reality my destination would be to my left. Needless to say, I clocked a lot of unnecessary miles on the car that year and used an exorbitant amount of fuel. Mom and Dad joked about it and called me "Wrong Way Corrigan". Douglas Corrigan was the pilot that had filed his flight plans from New York to Los Angeles, but ended up in Ireland due to heavy cloud cover and misread instruments. Many people thought his misdirection was intentional, as he had been previously denied the privilege of piloting a transatlantic flight. Regardless of intentional or not, he was coined "Wrong Way" for his escapade. After learning about Douglas Corrigan, I felt pretty good in comparison, knowing that I might have ventured to the next town before I realized I was heading in the wrong direction, but at least I stayed in the same state, not to mention the same country! Believe me, I was far from an adventurer when I drove behind the wheel, and I finally got my bearings and learned to navigate the small town of Ogden, Utah uneventfully and efficiently.

I was still sixteen years old when Robert and I met. He was already twenty at the time, and he lived upstairs from Mom, Dad and I on the third floor of our apartment complex with three other guys. Robert had moved to Utah four years earlier with his parents when he was still in high school. After finishing high school, he dabbled at college, not very seriously, though, and then got a job as an engineering assistant at Morton Thiokol, just north of Ogden. He worked in the engineering lab on the development of the solid rocket propellant for the space shuttle. As something of a fire bug by nature,

Robert enjoyed his job immensely and was continually amazed by the speed and temperature at which the substance burned as they tested it in the lab on a daily basis. Another thing the engineers studied during that time was the trajectory of a rubber band in flight. After Robert had worked there for six months, he had mastered the skill of shooting a fly off the television screen. I'm not talking about merely scaring the insect away by striking close to it; I'm referring to an ability to nail the pest dead-on through demonstrated pinpoint accuracy. He proudly displayed his prowess for as many houseguests as possible. Not many people can boast about learning new skills at work that enhance their leisure life as well, but even today, thirty years later, the fresh guts of a fly clinging to a precisely aimed rubber band brings a proud smile to Robert's face.

On New Year's Eve that winter, Robert called me, home from work, excited about the plans he had made for us that evening. He had asked his roommates, who were a few years older than him, to purchase a bottle of champagne for Robert and me to enjoy that evening. Robert himself had splurged on some steaks from the local butcher and prepared a lovely, intimate dinner for the two of us. After eating, some of our friends came over and we sat around visiting for hours, waiting for the clock to strike midnight. A few minutes before midnight, Robert emerged from his bedroom carrying a string of fire crackers and told everyone to head outside.

The weather was dreary and the skies had been dropping sleet all evening, but after a few glasses of champagne, I felt very warm and cozy, not to mention a little forgetful, and I went outside with neither my coat nor my shoes. I had on wool socks, so my feet stayed toasty. A thin layer of ice had frozen on the parking lot, but we didn't care. Robert divided up the firecrackers between himself and his two buddies while we gals stood around chatting, waiting for Robert to give the signal that the New Year had actually arrived. Robert began his countdown ten seconds before his watch read midnight, and a second after he said, "One," he shouted, "Happy New Year!" The guys, prepared as the countdown occurred, lit their firecrackers and the air was suddenly filled with loud explosions, followed by clouds of smoke. I looked around and saw several porch lights come on and thought, "Oh great, the neighbors will probably call the cops on us." Then I noticed Robert crouching down on the ground with his lighter, and asked him what he was doing; he explained that he had a small amount of rocket propellant glued to the top of one of those little army tanks that you can purchase at the fireworks store around the Fourth of July. I peered down at the tank, unable to see the alleged material and asked Robert where it was. He pointed to a little speck, about the size of a pinhead. I didn't say a word about it, but thought to myself that this stunt was going to be totally anticlimactic. Still concerned about the ruckus we had caused, I told him, knowing full well that the rocket propellant was not supposed to leave the confines of Morton Thiokol, that there may be a real possibility that the cops were on their way, since we had disturbed the entire neighborhood. A split second after the words left my mouth, the propellant lit volcanically, as if immediately reaching critical mass, and the little tank shot across the parking lot at amazing speed, not stopping until it was squarely positioned underneath a car, the volatile burn showing no signs of easing up. Realizing there was a distinct possibility that the ignited propellant could cause the car to catch on fire and not wanting to spend the night in jail, I decided it best if I disappeared into the apartment. Obviously, everyone else had decided upon the same strategy because all of our friends scampered towards the steps leading to the apartment. Trying to follow as quickly as I could, I quickly realized I had a small dilemma: my socks had frozen to the pavement, and I couldn't move an inch. In a panic, I pulled my feet out of the socks and ran barefoot over the frozen pavement, trying to escape detection. As we all high-tailed it up to the third floor, trying to flee undetected, I became painfully aware that we sounded like a herd of elephants tromping up the wooden staircase. Fortunately for Robert, and the rest of us, the propellant burned out and there was no lasting harm done. About ten o'clock the next morning, after the sun had been up for a couple of hours, I went outside and retrieved my socks, which now lay in a puddle that had formed as the sun thawed the ice from the storm the night before. Due to their ideal location, they had been run over by several vehicles during the course of the morning—which was similar to how I felt after a long night of consuming too much champagne.

Robert and I spent the next few years sharing our dreams openly while I finished high school and we married soon after I completed high school. We spent the next two years focused on working and his goal of racking up college credits. We knew it would take him at least four years to complete his degree, so we took it one day at a time. We both wanted a family, so we planned that he would complete his college education and then we would start a family. We both wanted to have two kids by the time we were thirty, and we knew if we stayed the course, we should have sufficient time to accomplish that goal. Robert wanted me to stay home and be a full-time mother once we had children, so since it took both of our earnings to make ends meet and pay for his education, the only reasonable plan consisted of us having children after he completed his degree. We knew that once he had that precious piece of paper, he could secure a job paying more than we both made at the time, earning enough to support us and two children. Back then, a family of four could actually be supported by one working parent.

Initially, when I realized my period was past due, I didn't panic. In fact, it took me almost three weeks to reach the dreaded conclusion that there was a very real possibility that our well-thought-out plan was about to go awry. We had been married for a little more than two years, and Robert was only halfway to achieving his goal of completing his college education. After visiting the doctor and receiving confirmation that I had a healthy fetus growing inside me, I called Robert and repeated five famously ominous words: "Houston, we have a problem."

Labor Day

Most people recognize Labor Day as a celebration of the social and economic achievements of the American worker. It represents the dedication of the labor unions and the advances they made in helping the American worker receive fair treatment in the workplace, as well as rewarding said workers with a lovely day off from actual labor. These sentiments are all well and good, familiar to most working Americans and more than a few happy schoolchildren, but to me, Labor Day represents something a little more personal: it's, in fact, a celebration of those two infamous days in history that I survived childbirth. I don't want to take anything away from history, and I am not trying to downplay the role that labor unions played in getting the American worker decent pay for a hard day's work. I do, however, know that I have never worked so hard in my life as I did on those two days in my history. Tara shares this opinion with a justifiably healthy vehemence.

Many women describe childbirth as an enriching experience, the ultimate achievement of womankind, but as a woman who experienced it firsthand, I can tell you that child-birth is about twice as rewarding as a tooth extraction, and a lot more painful. I hear other women portray pregnancy as the greatest time of their lives. They enjoy telling others about how they felt better than they had ever felt in their entire lives and how pregnancy was the absolute pinnacle of their existence here on earth. Personally, I think after you have had your belly stretched beyond all reasonable limits of nature and watched your hips slowly but inexorably inch towards the arms of an oversized recliner, you will probably never be the same again. Maybe that explains why every woman I meet remembers their first pregnancy with such fondness. It just happened to be the last time in her life that every part of her body was in the right place and looked halfway appealing in the nude.

Even though I withstood pregnancy uneventfully, I still would not in any way call it the best time of my life. I certainly didn't feel my best throughout what is essentially a cruel test of endurance, although I didn't suffer from morning sickness, so I guess it could have been worse. My back ached perpetually, and I had trouble sleeping at night because of it. Although, in retrospect, when compared to the several months after the birth of my children, I guess I slept great. My feet swelled regularly, which aggravated my already chronically troublesome feet, not to mention the fact that it is almost impossible not to waddle when you walked during your pregnancy; between my throbbing feet and my widening girth, I certainly waddled more than I walked. Nonetheless, despite all the annoyances that came with pregnancy, it wasn't the most memorable process in my life—just a necessary if bothersome moment on the path to motherhood. However, Labor Day told a completely different story.

Robert worked swing shift when I was pregnant with Eric, so I usually waited up for him to get home. One night after he arrived home, I prepared something for him to eat, and then we chatted for a little while before we went to bed. Usually, I wouldn't stay up that late with him, having to work in the morning, but I had just begun my six weeks of maternity leave and had decided to enjoy my leisure time. We finally settled into bed around 1:00 a.m. and around 3:00 a.m. I awoke to a squirt of water between my legs. That wasn't necessarily uncommon during my last trimester, since if I had more than an ounce of liquid in my bladder, I couldn't contain it. I hated sneezing when I was pregnant, because I didn't possess the capacity to sneeze without wetting myself. In fact, I went through an average of about six pairs of underwear each day during that time. (Thank God for Wal-Mart.)

I rolled over and got up out of bed. Every time I moved or took a step, water seeped out from between my legs. That's when I realized that it wasn't urine that dribbled out of my body, but amniotic fluid. I thought that when a woman's water broke, a big gush of water surged out of her body. In my case, the fluid just dripped here and there. Regardless of the rather less dramatic commencement of labor, I knew that I would end up in the hospital that day, so I gathered up all the dirty clothes in the house and started doing laundry. I assumed that I wouldn't be home for a couple of days, so I thought I would get some of the housework caught up before I went on my sojourn. Besides, I didn't want to rouse Robert yet, and I wasn't experiencing any labor pains, so I didn't anticipate an urgent need to leave for the hospital.

As I went about my work, little hunger pangs danced in my stomach, but one thing our instructor emphasized to us in Lamaze class was never, never eat if you expect your child's delivery that day. Of course, they told us a lot of things in Lamaze class that proved to be contrary to my experience, though I didn't know it at the time. Eric was born in 1980, and Robert and I, along with many middle-class couples of that time, had taken natural child-birthing classes prior to Eric's arrival. Many experts recommended natural childbirth as the preferred method of delivery, rather than surrendering and asking for drugs to numb the pain. I would almost bet that these so-called experts mainly consisted of men, who obviously had never experienced the mind-numbing pain of labor. But, as I said, I wasn't yet aware of the depth of pain I would eventually undergo and happily learned the many different techniques taught in class which allowed a woman to tolerate the labor pains naturally. The main thrust of the class centered on breathing. Deep, steady breaths would supposedly help you survive the ordeal. "Maintain focus", the instructor said, as the man continually rubbed your back and spoke softly to you in order to help you keep your concentration. The instructors also recommended that you take an object to the hospital that looked pleasant, so you had something reassuring and lovely on which to focus. Theoretically, you fixated on this object while practicing your breathing exercises and this assisted in maintaining your concentration. But it's here that I want to pause and, looking back from the other side of my experience, say something instructive and pointed about natural childbirth, especially in relation to delivering your first child: *it is a VERY BAD IDEA!*

Still, as always an obedient student, I naively decided to be a good patient and not eat anything that morning, because the instructors really stressed the importance of that issue. They repeated, emphatically, "No food or drink when you are about to have a baby, because you will just end up vomiting." That in itself didn't seem like a real pleasant experience, let alone when it might be simultaneous with the pain of labor. I puttered around the house until around 8:00 a.m., which was when Robert joined the conscious world and asked me what the heck I was doing. I told him that I felt fairly certain that we were going to have a baby that day, and he sprang out of bed in excitement. We hastily gathered up my over-night bag and, after stopping at the store to pick up some film, we got to St. Benedict's Hospital in Ogden, Utah, about 9:30 that morning. The date was September 24th, 1980.

We went directly to the labor and delivery area, although I really hadn't begun labor yet. Our Lamaze instructor told us that, when our water broke, we should immediately go to the hospital. So other than a few loads of laundry and a little housework, I followed directions almost to the letter. The nurse informed me of what I already knew— that my water had broken—and they planned to wait a few hours to see if I went into labor naturally. If not, they would induce labor with an intravenous drip. Personally, I didn't care what they did; I just wanted to have the baby and the sooner the better.

Just before noon, the nurses hooked me up to an I.V. drip that contained a drug called Pitocin, which facilitates dilation and induces labor. The I.V. administered so many drops per minute but my body didn't cooperate as well as I would have hoped. Each time the nurse came to check on me, she increased the dosage, and I dilated another centimeter and then stopped. This happened over and over, so by 6:00 or so that evening, I started getting a little irritated. Not really at the nurse, or the doctor, or Robert, or anyone in particular, just everyone in general. I think the pain of labor put me in the mood to kill someone. I think I became genuinely homicidal about that time, because around that time, the nursing staff decided to bring in a meal for Robert, since he had to be starving after being there all day without any food. Those bitches! Needless to say, my mood shifted from slightly irritated to downright pissed off in less than a minute. I couldn't believe that Robert had the nerve to sit there and eat in front of me, either, but he did. I remember the glands in my mouth immediately began having a water fight. I actually started to drool a little bit from smelling the food and watching Robert consume his meal, heartily and happily, as if I weren't lying right there next to him slowly starving to death in the midst of giving birth to his damned kid.

Robert could tell—once he had consumed every scrap of food in the joint and returned his attention to me—that I had started struggling with the pain, so he rummaged in the overnight bag and brought out good ol' Thumper. In case you haven't seen the movie *Bambi*, Thumper, the cute bunny rabbit who befriended Bambi, had a knack for saying the wrong thing. Robert had bought me a stuffed Thumper at Disneyland a couple of years earlier, and I have to say that I always thought Thumper looked completely adorable—fuzzy and soft, with big round eyes and a puffy little tail—in short, the perfect object on which to focus my ravaged attention. His charming face displayed a huge, welcoming smile and one of his big paws was cocked up in the air, just like in the movie when he repeatedly banged his foot on the ground.

Robert pulled Thumper out of my overnight bag and, with this stupid smile on his face, said, "Look at the bunny. C'mon, Sheryl, focus. Look at Thumper." The only thing I felt like doing at that point was killing someone; I felt like such crap that not even the most adorable stuffed animal in the world would get me to focus on anything but the pain. He tried to be firm, but I guess he realized he treaded on thin ice, since he had just eaten a full meal in front of me and my only meal of the night consisted of chipped ice. Admittedly, though, Robert had been letting me sip on his Pepsi that afternoon, even though that was against the rules. That small kindness might possibly be the only reason I allowed Robert to live that day. Unfortunately, the same can't be said for poor Thumper.

Stubbornly, Robert stood beside the bed, continuing to wiggle Thumper in front of my face, repeating himself, "Look at the bunny, Sheryl. Focus on your bunny." I have some advice for those of you who chose to try this idiotic form of torture. *Do not stand within arms' reach of a woman in labor.* Such foolhardy practice could wind up being very harmful to said perpetrator, a.k.a. torturer—the silly man holding the stupid object in the false hope that the woman in labor might actually be able to focus and breathe. Luckily for Robert, in our case, it was poor Thumper who got assaulted. I can't say that I fully remember every aspect of the moment I snatched that poor bunny out of Robert's hands. But I can tell you I remember ripping off his tail and hurling it across the room towards Robert, who quickly moved as far away from me as he could get, knowing he might possibly and quite probably be my next victim. The next thing I knew I had reduced poor Thumper to mere fabric and stuffing and violently flung his parts around the room while I screamed, "You look at the friggin bunny, you moron!"

That was the last time before Eric's birth that I saw Robert that evening. He promptly disappeared, and two nurses entered the room to attend to me from that point forward. The fact that they were trained professionals was a good thing, and I settled down a little bit after the incident. Around 9:00 that evening I was at last on the verge of having the baby. The two nurses scurried around the room, placing sterile blankets underneath me in preparation for the birth of my first child. I experienced some severe pain by that time, and I had to urinate something fierce. I told the nurse that I needed to get up and go to the bathroom. Thinking that I had completely lost my mind by that time, the nurse attempted explaining that the baby's weight pressed on my bladder. This pressure caused the sensation that made me feel as if I needed to relieve myself. I told her that, in fact, I needed to go, really, really bad, so I asked her to retrieve a bedpan for me or let me get up. I will never forget the look on that woman's face. The empathetic look of complete pity lead me to believe that she was convinced that I had gone completely insane. Of course, she didn't know the whole truth; she thought that all I had consumed that afternoon was my dinner of ice chips, when I had actually had a good serving of Pepsi, thanks to Robert. She came over to the side of the bed, patted me on the shoulder condescendingly, and said, "That's okay honey. Go ahead and go. It'll be okay."

That was all the affirmation that I needed and I let it loose. The urine immediately flowed out of me like someone had turned on a high-pressure hose. Once you turn it on, it isn't that easy to turn off. She pleaded loudly, "Stop! Stop! Let me get the bedpan!" It was too late by that point, because for once in the last ten hours, I felt good. It didn't last for very long, but I can tell you it was the only pleasant feeling I had that day, even if it only lasted a few seconds. Needless to say, the nurse had to change all the sterile blankets and redo everything she had worked on for the last ten minutes. I also must admit that I got a little pleasure out of causing her to have to redo everything. But I just innocently gazed at her, conveying an equally empathetic look of pity on my face, with the same dose of condescension she had directed at me, all the time thinking, "Gotcha!"

The birth of Eric went off without a hitch after that, and soon I became the proud mother of a baby boy. After the delivery, the nurses gently put him in my arms. Astonished at the cheesy white substance, called vernix, that covered his body, Robert and I rubbed it on our skin, amazed at its lubricating properties. Finally, the nurses came in and took Eric away to clean him up. Robert, being the considerate and gracious husband and now father, decided to capture the touching moment on film: the baby covered in white goo; my un-made-up face, slick with sweat and heavy from exhaustion; my hair jutting out from my head in all different directions. I looked ten times worse than I had ever looked in my life up to that point. I thanked him appropriately for preserving that precious moment in time for me to ponder at a later date.

Meanwhile, my stomach screamed for anything edible. The clock had passed 11:00 at night by that time and the nurse promptly informed me that the kitchen had closed many hours earlier. But, when she saw the look on my face, she quickly said that she would attempt to find me something to eat. I didn't really care what it was; I just wanted something in my stomach. After all, it had been more than 24 hours since I had anything to eat. A few minutes later she returned, carrying a plastic container with a bologna sandwich in it. I thought I had nearly made it to the pearly gates, because that sandwich looked like a miracle to me. It might have just been bologna, but my eyes saw a filet mignon. Before she had time to explain that the sandwich was all she could find, and of uncertain provenance, I had opened the container and started munching on the sandwich. Frankly, I didn't care if she had pulled it out of the trash because it looked perfectly edible to me—almost anything would've looked perfectly edible to me. I don't really know how old the sandwich was, but the edges of the bread felt like they had been toasted, while the middle of the bread had gone a little flaccid. The truth of the matter was that the sandwich must have been left over from lunch. The real question was from which day. I have eaten my share of day-old bread, and compared to that, I reckoned that this sandwich had to be at least a week old. Still, I chose to assume that someone had simply left it sitting out, uncovered, since lunch that day and so the edges had dried out and the middle had gotten squishy, probably from the mayonnaise. It consisted of two thin slices of Wonder bread, a slice of rubbery American cheese, and a slice of old bologna. I know it doesn't sound very appetizing, but I proclaim that it tasted like the best sandwich I ever had in my entire life. I know it sounds crazy, but I guess the combination of pain and starvation warps the mind. But no matter what the case, contentment finally passed over me, and my satisfied stomach allowed me to slip into slumber after a truly exhausting day. Of course, as soon as I fell asleep, I dreamt of that nurse standing just outside my door, chanting in a sing-song voice, "I pulled it out of the trash. I pulled it out of the trash. Gotcha back!"

I think it's curious that both Tara and I chose to deny the use of drugs during labor. Although we shared the same choice, our motivations came from two very different perspectives. Tara, who cringed at the thought of being in the hospital, let alone getting poked or cut, initially refused medication out of the fear of being stuck with a needle. She believed that a good enough possibility existed that she could suffer paralysis from having a needle incorrectly inserted into her spine to put her off such medication.

My motivations stemmed from a totally different perspective. I vehemently believed that if I ingested anything into my body that could in any way harm the fetus, it would. All the headlines at the time discussed natural childbirth and what wonderful benefits it provided, both for the child and the mother. Commonly, we both believed that our worst fears would come true if we took the easy road of medicating the pain. For Tara, the fear was paralysis, where my anxiety led me to imagine the baby would be harmed in some way. For either of us, it didn't matter how remote the possibility was, but instead that we traveled the safest path to motherhood.

Today, we both agree that our refusal of drugs sprang from ignorance and superstition. I think that my experience could have ultimately been a pleasurable memory had I chosen to moderate the pain through the use of medical science. Instead, we both chose to suffer out of fear that fate would somehow single us out. I usually conclude that I wouldn't change my past experiences even when the situation turns grave, because life is, quite simply, a learning escapade. But in the case of the first Labor Day, Tara and I both deduce that everyone, at some time in their life, makes a mistake they wish they could undo. I gave birth to two sons, Eric and Jess, while Tara had two girls, Tiffany and Heidi. It's not that we are dissatisfied with the outcome, since we each have two beautiful children resulting from those horrific days. It's that we wish we could have cherished the experience of labor instead of shuddering at the very thought of it.

On the Road Again

Tara and Jerry were stationed at Ft. Lewis, Washington when Jerry came home from work one day and told Tara that he had received orders for reassignment to Ft. Knox, Kentucky; they had two weeks to pack and head down the road. When Tara asked Jerry what his new orders were, he explained that his new assignment required him to work as a tank instructor. Jerry's response puzzled Tara, since Jerry had been working as a Black Hawk helicopter crew chief at the time. She didn't understand why the Army would assign Jerry a job in which he had no experience. Jerry said that he felt the Army wanted someone who had been in the service for a long time and had a lot of experience; it didn't matter on what type of equipment. Tara nodded in agreement, although his reasoning still didn't make a lot of sense to her. Then again, the Army didn't always make a lot of sense, in her experience.

Tara ran around for the next two weeks hectically. She gave notice at the bank where she worked and attempted to get everything in order for their move. This included not only packing their belongings, plotting a course, and readying the girls—Tiffany, who was five at the time, and Heidi, who had just turned two—but also budgeting for the trip. When the Army issues orders for a move, it provides a move allowance for the family, but it only releases a portion of their move pay initially, and the remaining allotment cannot be collected until the person reports to their assigned post. Before they left, Jerry collected the portion of pay allocated to him for the move, which wasn't very much, so Tara packed a picnic lunch so they didn't have to spend money on food during the first leg of their road trip. Staying with family along the way would also help out with expenses. She also packed some sugar packets, because, although Tara liked her coffee black, Jerry preferred his with sugar. Thus, she didn't have to fill two different thermos containers. Bright and early the next morning they set out on what would be a very long journey.

The plan was simple. On the first leg of the trip, they planned to drive straight through to Ogden, Utah, where Mom, Dad, and Robert and I lived at the time. From there, their next step would be New Albany, Indiana, where our grandparents lived, then on to Ft. Knox. As such, they wouldn't have to spend money on lodging. Tara knew the trip would be long and grueling, so she made sure that everyone had plenty of room. Tara and Jerry sat in the front seat of the Blazer, the girls sat in the back seat, and the dog and the cat lay comfortably in the hatchback. Since the Army commissioned a moving company to pack and transport the majority of the family's belongings and Tara was uncertain when or if they would ever be reunited, Tara and Jerry pulled a trailer with a Spitfire on it that they had fully packed with clothes and other essentials. After a long first day on the road, they stopped at a Mom & Pop store to get something to eat, since dusk began to fall, and all the picnic supplies had already been depleted. By that time Tara didn't care what the kids ate, she just wanted to get through the night.

When they climbed back into the Blazer, Tara tried to make the girls comfortable so they could get some sleep. She put Tiffany in the back seat lying down, and put Heidi on the floor, on top of most of the blankets; this would give her something soft to lie on and insulate her from the cold floor. It was winter and, although it was comfortable inside the Blazer, Tara wanted to make sure her youngest daughter stayed warm. It seemed that the girls had dozed off pretty quickly, as all was silent from the back seat. But about thirty minutes after they had refueled and left the Mom & Pop store, Tiffany started whining, "Mommy, my tummy hurts." Tara, being the sensitive mother, said, "Well, then, just be quiet and go back to sleep and then your tummy won't hurt anymore." A few minutes later, though, Tara heard Tiffany coughing, choking, and gagging. Suddenly, Heidi screamed, "Wwhhaaaaahhhh!" A rancid smell filled the car and Tara realized that Tiffany had vomited. Since Tara taught Tiffany not to throw up in the bed—the back seat in this case—Tiffany leaned over and puked on the floor, all over Heidi's head.

Keep in mind that, by now, darkness filled the car; Tara and Jerry had no water to clean up the mess, and no light to even see what damage had occurred. Tara told Jerry to pull off at the next exit so she could clean up the mess. The next exit just happened to be a weigh station that was closed for the night, but it did have a little light, emphasis on the word *little*. When Tara peered down at the damage, she saw that Tiffany had managed to fill Heidi's ear with vomit, and Heidi's head was pretty much covered in the foul stuff. The only thing that she had to clean Heidi up with was cold coffee; she felt thoroughly thankful that she hadn't put any sugar in it. All the blankets that Heidi had been laying on were also saturated with vomit, so Tara and Jerry stuffed them in a plastic garbage bag and threw them in the Spitfire.

Back on the road again, Tara very much looked forward to arriving in Ogden. The trip began to feel endless; at least, for now, the girls had settled in and slept quietly. Before she knew it, though, two o'clock rolled around. Although Tara herself felt exhausted, Jerry struggled not to fall asleep at the wheel, so he pulled over and let Tara drive. As Tara tried to accelerate, she realized that the Blazer wouldn't shift: apparently the transmission had started to fail. It seemed their journey got better with each mile. She quickly pulled over so Jerry could get out and assess the problem. As it was wintertime, Tara had donned a canary yellow ski parka, but Jerry, being the macho man that he claimed, said he didn't need a coat and wore just a rather thin, long-sleeved shirt with no jacket. Still, it was crucial that he get out of the warm car to determine if there was anything that he could do to get the Blazer to accelerate faster than 25 miles per hour—in the middle of the pitch-black night.

Tara knew that the temperature felt far too blustery for Jerry to survive out of the car for any length of time with no jacket or coat on, so she decided that the best course of action was for Jerry to wear her brightly colored, waist-length parka. He reluctantly acquiesced, so there he stood, on the side of the road, in the freezing cold darkness, wearing a canary yellow parka that ended about mid-abdomen, with sleeves that only covered three-quarters of his arms. After a brief investigation under the hood, Jerry decided that no course of action would alleviate the problem. By that time he was fully awake, and half frozen, so he regained control of the wheel.

Determined to get the Blazer moving at more than 25 miles per hour, Jerry pushed down firmly on the accelerator until the engine screamed. Tara felt certain that the engine would blow up about the time that the Blazer finally shifted. She became cautiously relieved since, one, the car had not actually blown up and, two, they could now travel at a blazing 40 miles per hour. Again, Jerry pushed the accelerator to the floor and the engine howled. Tara thought for sure he was going to destroy the car, which would leave them stranded, and she feared she'd have to derive an escape plan in case the car caught on fire. But then the transmission shifted again. Jerry felt like a savior. They traveled at a reasonable 60 miles per hour, and he decided they wouldn't stop for anything. About four hours outside of Ogden and with enough gas to get there, they drove straight through.

When they arrived in Ogden, Tara immediately handed Heidi to Mom and asked her to take care of the mess because she desperately needed sleep. After a couple of days of rest and relaxation while the transmission in the Blazer got repaired, they headed to Ft. Knox, Kentucky with an extra two hundred dollars of cash that Dad gave them. Tara felt lucky because Ft. Knox, Kentucky was only about an hour from where we grew up in New Albany, Indiana. Our grandparents still lived there and so Tara and her family would stay with them, since, after paying for the transmission, they had absolutely no cash left from their portion of the travel pay. At least they knew that when Jerry reported for duty, he would get the rest of the move pay.

Tara likes to refer to the trip from Washington to Utah as getting married all over again. When her and Jerry got married in Elko, Mom insisted that Tara had something old, something new, something borrowed and something blue. Tara breaks it down like this: the something old was the transmission in the Blazer, the something new was the new transmission in the Blazer, the something borrowed was the seed money Dad had loaned them, and the something blue, or as Tara puts it, someone blew as in Tiffany's vomiting ordeal. Needless to say they never renewed their wedding vows.

Unlike the trip to Ogden, the trip to New Albany occurred uneventfully. They arrived at our grandparents' house a week before Jerry's report date. They found a quaint little house and put down a whole $50 of earnest money in anticipation of buying it. Jerry went to Ft. Knox the morning of his new assignment start-date, and the officer on duty there immediately asked, "What are you doing here?" Jerry handed them his orders and the officer said, "You're a Black Hawk helicopter crew chief. You don't know anything about tanks. This doesn't make any sense!" Apparently, there had been a mistake in the issuance of Jerry's orders, so they proceeded to search the system for an assignment that more fittingly suited a Black Hawk helicopter crew chief. It appeared that the only opening was in Ft. Lewis, Washington, where they had just come from, but the officer promised to keep looking for something a little bit closer. The situation resembled a bad dream in excruciatingly slow motion, truly a nightmare. Meanwhile, as Tara and Jerry waited for him to receive another assignment, they had no money. Since Jerry couldn't report for duty, he could not collect the rest of his travel pay. Thank god for grandparents!

After waiting approximately two weeks, Jerry received orders to head to Ft. Eustis, Virginia. So they packed up what little belongings they had and hit the road again. The trip took them through the Blue Ridge Mountains, which looked quite captivating with their bluish hue. The steep, winding roads followed the edge of the mountain cliffs, which supplied them with a breathtaking view of the canyons below. As they approached the summit, a panorama of the entire countryside emerged. The virgin snow, pure white and piled high, sparkled as the sun glistened off the snowdrifts amassed along the side of the road. Tara admired the unspoiled perfection of the landscape and enjoyed the scenic road trip, relaxing for the first time in days. She sighed deeply, inhaling the clean mountain air, and smiled. This most pleasurable excursion was a welcome relief from the hustle and chaos of the previous weeks.

Suddenly, without warning, one of the tires on the trailer separated from the axle, and Tara, jolted out of her reverie, watched it roll past them. As the Blazer swerved fiercely, Jerry frantically tried to prevent the trailer from jack-knifing, and fought to slow the momentum of the trailer so that all their worldly belongings wouldn't go somersaulting downhill. As the Blazer eventually rolled to a stationary position, they watched in horror as the wayward tire hit a rock and became airborne. Normally, this would not have been such a big deal, but since the tire headed straight down a steep grade, for every foot it bounced up, it had five or six feet to fall before it reconnected with planet earth. The tire took on a life of its own that afternoon, on a mighty trek to freedom. Every time it landed, it bounced even higher. Tara spotted a blind curve toward which the tire inevitably bounded and prayed that a vehicle would not appear around the corner. With the energy it had gained, that tire could easily cause a fatal accident. Finally, it bounded to the base of a hill, bounced up against the side of the mountain, and came to rest at the bottom. Both Tara and Jerry sighed with relief.

The question then became *what in the heck were they going to do now?* They had two kids, a dog and a cat, a broken trailer, and a stray tire that rested a good walking distance down the side of a mountain. Carefully, Jerry jockeyed the trailer and the Blazer off the road and onto the shoulder, so that he could assess the damage safely. He realized that the axle of the trailer was no longer attached. The U-bolts had sheared off of their base. So he unhooked the trailer on the side of the road. The two of them agreed on a plan. Jerry would go find the necessary supplies to fix the trailer, taking the girls with him, while Tara stayed with the trailer, keeping the dog for protection. Another important detail: it happened to be a Sunday.

Tara sat on the side of the road, perched on the tire that they had retrieved, with the dog close by. Not more than five minutes passed after Jerry left that a State Trooper stopped to inquire why Tara sat on a tire on the side of the road with just a dog for company. Tara relayed the story, and the Trooper was convinced that he could find Jerry. After all, he drove a red Blazer with Oregon plates on it. How many vehicles with that combination could be around that immediate location? The Trooper was familiar with the facilities at the next exit, and since he knew the town had only one store that Jerry could possibly be at, he hurriedly went on his way to see if he could be of assistance.

The State Trooper located Jerry, and although the store didn't have exactly what Jerry needed, Jerry managed to fix the axle with a chain and some new bolts. Even though the repair job was makeshift, Jerry felt certain it would sustain them until they arrived in Virginia. Of course, they had to remove the Spitfire from the trailer, because with a broken axle, the trailer couldn't handle the extra weight. To make matters even more complicated, they had to unload the Spitfire on the side of the road and put all their precious belongings in the back seat of the Blazer. Tara drove the Spitfire, and Jerry drove the Blazer with the empty trailer behind it. The rest of the trip occurred fairly uneventful, but really, after that, what wouldn't be?

If you think the story ended there, you'd be wrong. Once they arrived, the house hunting started all over again near Ft. Eustis, Virginia. All of the houses that they located allowed children or pets, but not both. Given the choice of giving up their children or their pets, Tara and Jerry decided to keep them both. Previously unbeknownst to them, Jerry's Mom had decided to buy a house in that area as an investment. When they found out, they were relieved and thankful that, when asked, Jerry's Mom offered them her house. It was in Chesapeake, Virginia. The house had sat vacant for four years and looked filthy, but Tara and Jerry didn't complain, since they were allowed to keep their pets *and* their children.

After they started moving in, they discovered that the water pipes hadn't been drained before the last resident moved out. Thus, every time Tara turned on the water, the pipes sprung a new leak. Tara busily cleaned the upstairs bathroom, and after finishing, she turned off the water. She noticed that the faint hissing sound usually present when the water is turned on didn't fade when she turned the faucet to the off position. But, being unfamiliar with the new house, she didn't think too much of it. Until, that is, Jerry started screaming from the first floor, "Turn off the water! Tara, turn off the water!" Tara ran downstairs and saw that water gushed out of the ceiling. Jerry still yelled at her to turn the damn water off, but Tara just shrugged her shoulders, not knowing what she could do, since she already had turned off the water.

For the following week, Tara cleaned, scrubbing every surface and removing layers of grime, dust, and various other substances that had made their way throughout the vacant house for so long. While Tara cleaned, Jerry patched cracks in the pipes, one by one. They both labored constantly, just about every waking hour, for a week.

The day that they finally got everything moved in, the house was clean and all the pipes were repaired. Just as they got the last of their stuff into the house, the owner called and told them to vacate the premises. Apparently, the deal between Jerry's mother and the owner had taken a turn for the worst, and the purchase collapsed. In addition to this news, Tara and Jerry's bank account remained empty, because Jerry still had not reported for duty, and so they returned back to square one.

Fortunately, they found a house in the same neighborhood that was for rent, and although they had to paint the whole place, the owner allowed pets *and* children. After the owner provided the paint, Tara and Jerry painted the house and moved in. They used the trailer, still with the axle chained up, to move their furniture and belongings to the new house. Tara said they received several bizarre stares as they drove through the neighborhood with a washer or a couch on the trailer.

When Jerry reported to work the following week, he finally received the rest of his travel pay and they could eat again. Although the whole ordeal was a harrowing experience, it really made them appreciate the moments when things happen smoothly. Through our experiences, Tara and I have grown to respect the uneventful, even when the situation becomes boring. But even more important, we have learned to laugh at the absurd, such as Tara and Jerry's move to Virginia. If we didn't, we would both live miserable existences with our history of misfortune. We both agree that it doesn't matter what ingredients make the cake, it's how it tastes when it's complete. And just like a cake, life tastes sweet.

Diamonds Aren't a Boy's Best Friend

Babies smell sweet and feel soft and cuddly, although demanding at times, but for the most part are fairly simple to raise and care for. The fun part for parents doesn't begin until their children learn to walk and talk. However amusing the events may seem years later, as the events unfold, they may present somewhat of a challenge for the parents. When Eric first started to say a few random words, I felt thrilled beyond belief. The thought of actually communicating with him with something other than grunts was a tremendous relief, that is, until he learned the word why. Don't get me wrong, I have questioned many parental decisions that I've made throughout the years, but it becomes unsettling when your children begin to question them as well. A frequent conversation that Eric and I had during that time went something like this:

Me: "Eric, stop doing that."

Eric: "Why?"

Me: "Because I don't want you to get hurt."

Eric: "Why?"

Me: "Because you will cry."

Eric: "Why?"

Me: "Because it will hurt."

Eric: "Why?"

Me: "I don't know. I'm not a doctor."

Eric: "Why?"

Me: "Because I didn't get a medical degree."

Eric: "Why?"

Me: "Because I'm not that smart or that rich."

Eric: "Why?"

Me: "I don't know."

Eric: "Why?"

Me: "Never mind, go ahead and do it."

Since many times those conversations made me question my ability to actually raise children, I find it comforting, and surprising, that both my sons and I survived their rearing. Although along the way, all three of us had some bumpy patches in our journey to their adulthood.

During my pregnancy with Eric, my girlfriend Cindy called and suggested we all go to the movies. A new movie had opened that day called *Alien* (you might be familiar with it). The name didn't intrigue me, initially. I had a vision in my head of a movie similar to the old television show, *My Favorite Martian*, but I said, "What the heck! I'm game." I don't know if you've seen *Alien*, but it did not resemble *My Favorite Martian* in the least. The creature in *Alien* was black, grey, and slimy, and he stood upright on his two back feet. A long tail protruded off the end of his spine in sections, as if his vertebrae continued all the way to the tip. His head resembled an oblong eggplant (or a very large, half-limp penis) that extended back from his neck. But most frighteningly of all, not only did he have enormous primary teeth, he had a second set that slid forward, as if on a hinge, when he opened his mouth. The movement reminded me of when the teller pushes the drawer out to you for your deposit when you go through the drive-up window at the bank. Still today, *Alien* remains one of the scariest movies I have ever seen. Being horror film fanatics, Robert and I loved it.

After Eric's birth, *Alien* came out on video, and of course we had to rent it, watching it for a second, then a third time. My favorite part of the movie was after one of the crew members, who just happened to be male, had been inseminated with an alien egg, he slept for days. Upon wakening, he ate voraciously and suddenly began choking and convulsing. After several failed attempts, the baby alien violently burst through his skin and emerged from his stomach, screeching loudly as he exited his womb. I found satisfaction in knowing that finally a man got to experience the pain of natural childbirth.

I happened to talk to Tara that weekend and mentioned to her how much we both loved the movie. So, for Christmas the following year, Tara sent Robert an Alien figure, thinking it would be the perfect present. I don't know if you ever saw one of these figures, but it stood about 18" tall and looked just as hideous as the one in the movie. Naturally, Robert couldn't resist scaring Eric with it (another hallmark of male genetic material: the irrepressible urge to tease their children). When something appears unnaturally horrific, even two-year old children have enough sense to be frightened of it, and Eric was terrified of the Alien. Robert would run after him, shaking the Alien figure, and Eric would shriek and tear off and eventually end up behind my legs, crying. After a few days of this, I became highly irritated at Robert for scaring Eric with the creature.

Determined to end the madness and knowing that Eric trusted me—after all, I was his mother—I took the Alien from Robert and started stroking its hideous head, as if it were a puppy. I spoke sweetly to the Alien and kissed it on the mouth to show Eric it wouldn't, and couldn't, do him harm. Fairly quickly, Eric warmed up to the Alien and started stroking it and kissing it; soon, they became inseparable.

As Eric walked through the house, he dragged the Alien by his tail. They went everywhere together, and Eric even took the Alien to bed with him every night and slept with him. (That gives a whole new meaning to sweet dreams.) I didn't have to worry about the bed bugs biting because no bug in his right mind would get in bed with that abomination.

The next Easter when we talked about the Easter Bunny coming to visit, Eric started referring to him as the Beaster Bunny. I can't imagine where that came from. And when I started getting a visual image in my mind about what the Beaster Bunny might resemble, I choose to think of other, more pleasant thoughts. But I am sure he was a distant cousin of Eric's best friend, the Alien. Eric finally outgrew his infatuation with the Alien over time, but remains a fan of horror movie mania. I believe that my intentions were good at the time, but today—watching Eric encourage his own kids to play with bugs and skulls and the like—I wonder who is more responsible for the neuroses of our children, Robert or me.

Tara and I never lived close to one another while our children grew up. While I didn't get to see my nieces and she didn't get to see her nephews very often, one of our favorite pastimes consisted of talking on the phone and sharing funny stories about the kids. Another of my favorite stories is about the Mother's Day when Eric was eight years old and Jess was five. Jess has always loved helping out in the kitchen, and I still think that he has a chance to become a famous chef someday, but let me tell you, he had a rocky start.

Jess wanted to surprise me with breakfast in bed. He and Eric decided that they would make me an omelet for breakfast and deliver it to me in bed for Mother's Day. Out of the corners of my consciousness, I thought I heard a bit of a racket in the kitchen; a small part of my sleep-fogged mind thought briefly about the noise, but the rest of me was more interested in sleeping just a while longer. When I finally did wake up, Jess and Eric stood next to the bed, eagerly waiting for me to open my eyes and holding a plate containing an entirely unrecognizable substance. The concoction was a black and yellow conglomeration of many unsuitably paired ingredients. I distinguished that it included eggs, and I saw chunks of hot dogs buried in the mess, as well; some of it, though, looked unrecognizable and, for that, I felt grateful. Jess had an enormous grin on his face that I clearly remember to this day. He beamed like a little ray of sunshine. While trying to determine what the secret breakfast fully consisted of, I was concerned that if I asked, "What the hell is it?" I would hurt their feelings. I said, "Oh, thank you! What a wonderful surprise!" Knowing all along the term "surprise" was an understatement. I elbowed Robert and told him to wake up, because I knew that I urgently needed someone's help with consuming the mystery meal.

A vision kept appearing in my head of the Dr. Seuss book *Green Eggs and Ham*. When Sam's reluctant friend got ready to take a bite out of the titular dish, a doomed look covered his face. I felt this poor guy's pain that Mother's Day, but tried desperately not to show it. Jess held the plate proudly with his little out-stretched arms; all the while it seemed as if the edges of his smile reached all the way to each ear. I bravely took the plate from him, and he handed me a fork. I thought that if a make-believe creature can muster up enough courage to eat green eggs, I could manage to eat something, although unrecognizable, that was prepared by my own flesh and blood. I had thought it looked pretty bad from a distance, but after closer inspection, I knew eating it would be an even more difficult task than I originally imagined. Jess said, "Mommy, we made you an omelet for breakfast!" I could see some black chunks on the eggs, and I finally broke down and asked the boys what the omelet contained. Eric said it was a hot dog omelet. He said they had a little trouble cooking it because it began burning in the skillet while the middle remained runny. To compensate for the problem, they put it in the microwave for a couple of minutes. I thought, "Oh, so *that* explains the rubbery texture." I took a bite. It was difficult distinguishing the flavors over the strong taste of salt, but I soon realized that, in addition to hot dogs, it also contained mustard, ketchup, and pickles. Knowing that Robert favored salty foods, I decided that this was a task only he could complete. I said, "Yum! Here, Robert, try this!" Even he had difficulty with the level of salt, but all the while pretended that it tasted like a culinary delight. I thought about, accidentally on purpose, letting the omelet slide off the plate and onto the floor, and then taking the kids to McDonald's to make up for it. But I was concerned the omelet might bounce out of control and either hurt someone or break something, so I ultimately decided against it.

It seems that eight and five are really good ages for the creation of oft-repeated family stories. When my boys were those ages, we lived in Southern California and felt the need to involve the boys in sports; they needed exercise, fresh air, and some life lessons about team work. Therefore, we enrolled them in Little League Baseball. Eric was at a bit of a disadvantage, since most of the boys (and girls, for that matter) had already been playing for a couple of years by the age of eight. Eric went directly into C-Ball, in which the kids pitch to the batter. He performed fine after he got over his fascination with how the dust rose from the field as he scuffed his feet back and forth, all the while closely examining the stitching on his glove. He became quite the little leaguer, as he had a good eye at bat. He eventually played third base consistently and participated in practically all of the games his team played.

Jess, however, was another story. He started in T-ball, where the kids hit the ball off a platform called a Tee. For the first practice game, we congregated in a field with four bases and a pitcher's mound. I was never quite sure what the mound was for, since at that age the kids didn't pitch to the batter. They just stood on the mound waiting for a ball to roll towards them. I always thought that was kind of cruel, since often times the ball flew right to them, or should I say, right *at* them. Younger children typically don't possess quick reflexes and so can't react quickly enough to avoid being struck by the ball. But, adults and parents take a lot for granted when it comes to kids, and I know I certainly did when it came to Jess's understanding of the game.

Jess proudly strutted to the plate for his turn with the bat. He had a hard time positioning himself, since most of the time he only had one hand on the bat. The other hand waved furiously at me in the stands, while he displayed a huge smile on his face. As the team practiced, all of the parents knew we needed to be patient. Every time Jess swung, the bat hit the Tee and the ball fell to the ground. Jess had (still does have) a tender heart, and he became visibly frustrated. Finally, he swung the bat with all his might and made solid contact with the ball. It flew past the faux pitcher, the short stop, and into the outfield. Jess stood there beaming, proudly demonstrating his pleasure by grinning from ear to ear. I jumped out of my seat and yelled, "Run Jess, run!" Off he went to first base. He maintained a relaxed gait. Every four or five strides he searched the stands until he saw me and, with that same huge smile on his face, he would stop, lift his right hand, and wave enthusiastically at me. It seemed like an eternity, but finally, he reached first base. The boy in the outfield still chased the ball, so I screamed like a maniac, "Jess, run! Go to second, Jess, go! Run!" Off he went to second base, with that same *I have all day* stride, always searching for me in the stands and waving proudly. You would have thought he was Babe Ruth, and I think he might've imagined he was. When he reached second base, he stopped on the plate. I looked at the boy in the outfield as he tried picking up the ball and throwing it, but he just couldn't get a firm grip on the ball. It was as if the ball had a good coating of oil on it. Each time he attempted to throw it, the ball dropped at his feet. I shot out of the bleachers and ran along the sidelines screaming, "Jess, run! Go to third! Run now!" Off he went to third base, his smile widening with every stride and his little hand waving wildly. Evidently, he harbored visions of being on the All-Star team. When I looked to the outfield, a couple of other kids had joined the one boy who tried desperately to field the ball. One of the kids picked up the ball and threw it further out, and then they all ran after it. The coach sweated profusely, probably wishing she had never signed up for this task. Jess finally reached third base and he beamed with pleasure. I thought his little chest might pop. He breathed rapidly and I saw his chest rising and then falling with every breath. I knew that he could easily reach home plate at this point so I shrieked at the top of my lungs, "Jess, don't stop! Run, Jess, run!"

I never thought for a moment that Jess might not understand the basic rules of the game. That is, not until that moment, when, instead of completing his home run, Jess made a beeline for first base. As he ran over the pitcher's mound towards first base, the whole team started yelling, "No, Jess, go home! Go home!" A forlorn and puzzled look washed over his face as Jess continued running straight for first base. I acted like a complete maniac and wailed, "Go home, Jess! Run to home base!" Jess stopped in his tracks, started crying, ripped off his helmet, and with his head hung low, ran towards me. He looked up at me and said he wanted to go home. I was shocked. He seemed to be having such a good time up to this point. I said, "You can't go home, sweetie. You came here to play!" He said that no one wanted him to play, because everyone kept telling him to go home. I felt awful that he didn't know what home plate was, so as the other team still frantically tried to field the ball, I explained the basic rules of the game. When Jess finally realized that everyone meant for him to run to home plate, he quickly strutted over to home plate and stomped his foot proudly. The crowd roared and the rest is history!

Another piece of advice I'd like to proffer is about fund-raisers. You might be disinclined to accept advice from me at this point, having witnessed some of the more psychotic episodes in my life, but, trust me: this advice is *important*, key to every parent's sanity, so read carefully. When Jess and Eric participated in Little League, we went to practice one evening where the coach informed us that we were kicking off the annual fund-raiser. The idea seemed worthwhile, since many children's parents cannot afford to pay all the costs associated with having their kids play baseball. Personally, when we first put the boys in Little League, I thought you just had to show up. I didn't realize the expense that would be incurred for the uniforms and other sundries that the family had to pay for. Luckily, Robert and I could afford to pay for these items, but many parents could not. For those children, the League picked up the bill. Thus, the fund-raiser was born.

Don't get me wrong: I truly think that fund-raisers are a worthy cause. I believe that those who can afford certain things in life should help the others who can't. I also believe that any child who desires to participate in the game should be able to. I admit that maybe I got a little overzealous when I learned that they expected us to sell items to help the League stay solvent. After all, *it was for the children.*

The coach brought out a box filled with candy bars, that year's fund-raising item. Each child had a quota to sell two cases of candy bars, and since each case contained 36 candy bars, that meant that each kid had to sell at least 72 bars to meet our goal. Robert and I had *two* boys in Little League, of course, so we had to sell *four* cases of candy bars. I didn't think that sounded like too terribly many candy bars, and they only cost $1 each, so I initially felt excited about helping out the League. Plus, I thought it would teach the boys a valuable lesson: the way to pay for the things you want in life is to earn the money necessary to fund them.

Inspired by the chance to teach the boys about working for what you want, while at the same time also assisting the League, I made a deal with them. For every candy bar that they sold, I would sell one at work. I didn't just want to sell the candy for them, because I felt it was important for them to work towards their goals. But I definitely wanted to help. So at the time, this seemed to be the best of both worlds. I promised to take them door-to-door selling candy bars, and then I would take the same amount to work and sell them there. The League would benefit from both sales.

Initially, the boys didn't warm up to the idea of knocking on doors and asking strangers if they wanted to buy a candy bar in support Little League. However, the League threw in an incentive. The boy or girl who sold the most cases of candy won a prize of their choice, and so did the second-place runner-up, the third- and fourth-place winners, and so on. The exercise didn't solely consist of raising funds for the League; the children that sold the most received prizes. That carrot was all it took for them to get interested. They didn't know—or, really, care very much about—what the prizes might be; all they had to know was that the even remotest potential existed for them to win something great.

We arose that following Saturday morning, ready to go make some money for a worthy cause. I dressed the boys in their Little League uniforms for maximum effect and decided to drive them down the road to an apartment complex, so we could cover the most distance in the least amount of time. I had eight cases of candy bars in the back of my van, four for them to sell and four for me to take to work. The first couple of doors posed difficulties for the boys. Their shyness made it difficult for them to approach people and ask if they wanted to buy a candy bar to support Little League. As their mother, I thought they looked adorable in their outfits, and it seemed that the people answering the doors thought so also. Shyness and hesitation aside, they started selling candy right and left. I made the boys go up to the door by themselves while I stood in the background observing. Everyone smiled and generously handed the boys cash, and before we finished with the first building, we had breached the second case of candy bars.

I stood in the background and thought, "This is almost too easy." But I also felt pleased that they were having a successful experience. With every door, I observed their confidence building and that brought a smile to my face. Self-esteem is so important for kids of any age and I was pleased that the day turned into a good experience for them. I also knew that it wouldn't be too long before their four cases were sold and we could go home. The apartment complex consisted of eight buildings, and I can confirm that the boys knocked on every door. By the time we went home that evening, every single candy bar that was in the back of my van had been sold, and they felt excited. I never intended for them to sell all eight cases, but didn't want to put a damper on their successful quest. After all, *it was for the League*.

Needless to say, when we got home, Robert and I had a long talk and tried plotting our strategy: how in the heck were we going to sell eight cases of candy bars to our colleagues at work? The next day I called the coach and got another eight cases of candy bars. The coach, naturally, acted thrilled. I hadn't quite reached the panic stage, but became seriously worried about having to purchase whole cases of candy bars that I didn't want. The plan involved Robert taking a case to work and selling it, as would I, and then repeating the process until the candy disappeared. We had only two weeks to sell the bars, so even though the song "The Impossible Dream" kept running through my head, I kept my composure and attempted to convince Robert that we could actually accomplish the task.

I asked everyone I knew to buy a candy bar and even put a box in the coffee room with an envelope that said, "Only $1 to help your local Little League." This was my approach throughout the first week, but at that point we had managed to sell only four cases of candy bars. I calculated the cost of buying the last four cases of candy bars in preparation of our failure. You would think that getting rid of four cases in one week would be encouraging, since we still had another week to sell them. But the majority of the sales occurred in the first three days. After that, there may have been a dollar or two collected, but obviously the desire to help the local Little League faded fast among my co-workers. Robert surrendered totally and brought the rest of his bars home and told me that he gave up. He was a little irritated at me for making the pact with the boys in the first place, since apparently they performed much better at selling candy than we did.

I tried formulating a different plan of how we could sell the last four cases of candy bars, but Robert and I both worked most of the day. No other available time existed to devote to charitable causes. As I sat frowning at my desk one day, my girlfriend Linda walked up and asked me why I felt sad. I said, rather desperately, "Linda, you have to help me. I have four cases of candy bars to sell in the next three days." She told me that she would help, that on our lunch hour we would go around to various people at their desks and ask them point-blank if they wanted to buy a candy bar, the theory being that people found it harder to refuse when confronted face-to-face. I knew that it was a long shot, but at that point, I would willingly try anything.

At promptly 12:00 noon that day, she walked up to my desk with a big smile on her face. I had brought two cases of candy bars in that morning, hoping that we could sell as many as possible, figuring I would just purchase the rest. I grabbed a box and so did she. I said, "No, let's just take this case for today, and if we can sell these, we'll work on the other one tomorrow." She looked at me out of the corner of her eye and said, "I thought you said you had to sell four more cases?" I told her that I did, but that I would be satisfied if we could to unload at least two of them. She said, "Come on, girl. *We are going to sell these candy bars.*" She headed off with the case of candy bars on her hip, and I followed closely behind with my case in hand.

We rounded the first corner in the office building and there sat our first victim. She sat at her desk eating her lunch. Linda walked up to her and said, "Would you like to buy a candy bar to support your local Little League?" The woman agreed and dug a dollar out of her pocket and Linda gave her a candy bar. Not everyone ate lunch in the building, but quite a few people did, and we worked in an eight-story building. Thus, there were plenty of people that we could approach. Linda squarely walked up to them, unhesitatingly asked them to support their local Little League, and they promptly gave her a dollar for a candy bar.

When Linda was about halfway through her case of candy bars, she approached an older man at his desk. She held out a candy bar and said, "Would you like to buy a candy bar for $1 to support your local Little League?" He looked up at her and said, "No thanks, I don't eat candy." Linda immediately thrust the candy bar towards this man and screamed, "GIVE ME A DOLLAR!! IT'S JUST A DOLLAR!!" The guy quickly dug in his pocket, and before I fully realized what happened, handed her *two* bucks. I guess he wanted to be on the safe side and avoid direct physical confrontation. Linda just smiled sweetly and said, "Little League thanks you!" The incident, although entertaining, made me nervous. The rest of the day I frequently glanced over my shoulder, waiting to be escorted out by Security.

It wasn't difficult for Linda to sell four cases of candy bars, and in fact, it only took her two more days to get rid of the surplus in the back of my van. I chuckle when I look back over the situation. The boys, dressed up in their Little League uniforms, knocked on doors and smiled innocently, as they timidly asked if people wanted to buy a candy bar. And then, in contrast, there was a lady in a business suit and high heels, strong-arming co-workers to pitch in to help the community. Talk about covering both ends of the fund-raising spectrum. I really never thought in a million years that my boys would become so motivated about selling the candy bars. As a parent, I tried instilling in my children that they could do anything they wanted to do. They just had to stick with it. It wasn't that I didn't think they could sell those bars; I just didn't think they would. But I learned a valuable lesson during that episode: never underestimate your children, especially when a popular video game system is rumored to be involved. The boys did, by the way, win first prize that year: a Nintendo game system. Even today, they continue to amaze me (not that I'm proud of them or anything like that!). I can freely admit, though, that the mere mention of the term "fundraiser" still causes me to break out in hives and sprint in the opposite direction. I think I've become allergic.

One to Fifteen Odds Aren't Good

As my stories have invariably revealed, family is most important to Tara and me, and family get-togethers provide the highlights of our memories. For Christmas, 1989, our nomadic family decided to make an appearance back home in Indiana. It just happened to be one of the coldest Christmas seasons on record at the time. Mom and Dad lived in Wyoming; my family lived in California; and Tara's family lived in Virginia. I guess Dad passed the adventurous gene to both Tara and me. In fact, this genetic anomaly that leads to such distances between family members may be a big reason why our family gets along so well, since we don't have to put up with each other very often. Robert and I arrived early that Christmas, with our two boys in tow, and shortly thereafter, Tara, who had recently remarried after her divorce, showed up with her new husband Pete and her clan. Pete came with baggage, two teenaged kids, a boy and a girl, plus Tara's two girls. Mom and Dad were already at Grandpa and Grandma's house, along with my Uncle Wayne.

A total of fifteen people trying to cohabitate in a three-bedroom house for a week ended up being quite challenging. The term "cozy" is an extreme understatement. God forbid you had to get up in the middle of the night to go to the one bathroom available in the aging house. My grandparents and my Uncle Wayne had lived in that house almost 50 years, and one bathroom was normally sufficient for the three of them and any company or family who stopped by for a short visit. Aunt Joyce and Uncle Donny lived around the corner on the next street over, so they dropped by fairly often. But in these cases, they only accommodated a couple of extra people for a few hours at most. In our case that Christmas, that little bathroom had to accommodate fifteen people *round the clock*. Any time the line to the bathroom got too long, the one who could hold it the longest got to walk around the block to Joyce and Donny's so they could take care of business there. The situation at the grandparents' house only became more pronounced if you required the use of the single facility in the middle of the night: essentially, you had to take your life—and the lives of the children—into your own hands. In other words, you had to *run the gauntlet.* Have you ever tried to traverse a room with half a dozen children sprawled out on the floor? The tight housing conditions required that the kids sleep in and among blankets and sleeping bags on the floors of the living room and the hallway. So, you had to pick your way very carefully through the bodies to avoid tripping and falling and killing yourself or flat-out mashing one of the kids. Have you ever seen a person under the age of 18 sleep? Well, in case you haven't, I can tell you that they don't sleep in a straight line. I think their goal during the night is to take up every bit of space available, and then some. Not only do you have to try and avoid stepping on a stray hand or tripping over a leg, usually about the time you have found a safe spot for your next step, someone moves and you have to start searching all over again. If you actually make it to the bathroom successfully, even at 3:00 in the morning, chances are someone else will already be in there. In fact, you could even consider yourself extremely lucky if there wasn't a line.

The next morning, after waiting for over an hour to brush my teeth and realizing there was no way to get 15 minutes alone in the bathroom to take a shower, I decided, with the full support of Tara, that this arrangement was not copasetic for our families. (Not to mention that one of us was destined to come down with a bladder infection from having to hold it all the time.) As for the rest of our clan, we all know that kids don't need a good reason to bicker and fight, so we knew that continuing this arrangement would only add to the innate tension that runs through sibling blood. The bottom line was we didn't want to give them any more reasons to argue, and the tight living conditions clearly presented the perfect situation for them to get on each other's nerves.

So we called Grandma Nola, who temporarily lived with Aunt Florence and Uncle Dale since she fell and broke her hip, as we heard through the grapevine. We could already picture the neon-green VACANCY sign beckoning from front of her house. She had a fairly large house in the country, with four bedrooms and, best of all, TWO bathrooms. (Isn't it funny how you take some of the most important facilities for granted?) We called her and she said, no problem, we could make ourselves at home. We couldn't get there soon enough, so Uncle Dale met us there to make sure the pipes hadn't frozen and the furnace would kick on.

Grandma Nola's house felt almost like paradise after the close quarters of Grandma Grace's place. There were a couple of minor catches, of course (because why else would I be telling the story?). For one, because the house was out in the country, it sat amongst a myriad of critters. As many people know, that ubiquitous country critter, the flea, can lie dormant for months. That is, until someone disturbes them. Frankly, ten people tromping across the carpet was definitely enough to constitute a wake-up call; I really couldn't blame the poor devils for jumping up and taking notice. Not such a big deal, I suppose, but I happen to be highly allergic to fleabites. Tara has a slightly unfavorable reaction to the bites, as well, but not to the extent that I do. Even so, I can tell you it was still better than standing in a long line or picking your way through a pile of sleeping bodies to use the facilities at Grandma Grace's.

To take our minds off the minor discomforts, we thought we'd strike up a game of cards. As mentioned, the members of our family are avid card players (see previous for such infamous examples of said obsession as Grandma Grace and Mom destroying dozens of decks of cards). As Tara and I grew up, we played cards as a regular leisure-time activity. We knew how to play Rook and Pinochle at a very young age, and by the time we hit double digits, we could play as well as, if not better than, most adults. As a result, Tara likes to refer to us by telling other people that "we were born with a deck of cards in our hands." People who don't relate to cards tend to stare with an inquisitive but puzzled look on their face after hearing this. It's a sick form of amusement for Tara and me, while we watch these people actually trying to picture in their minds a newborn baby coming through the birth canal, clinging desperately to a deck of playing cards.

Anyway, to make a short story even longer, Tara, Robert, Pete, and I proceeded to sit at the kitchen table and commence with the nightly game of cards. As the night wore on, Tara and I would flinch about every couple of minutes, slapping our arms and legs. The guys looked at us like we acted crazy until I explained that we must've drummed up an army of dormant fleas. Each time the little bloodsuckers took a bite out of us we'd jump and then we itched like all get-out afterwards. Of course, the fleas didn't bother the guys, and they insensitively found our behavior quite amusing, but by the time the week ended, I looked like I had suffered from a severe case of the chicken pox. Still, given the two choices of lodging we had at the time, the chicken pox alternative didn't seem so bad.

Daily activities commenced every morning, as we drove into town to see our relatives. We enjoyed seeing everyone, since we only got together about once every six or seven years. But we still looked forward with anticipation to our more private nightly battle of the sexes at the card table over at Nola's. The second night we spent there, Pete came out of the bathroom during a much-needed break and announced that the toilet backed up. Since Pete stands around 6'2" and weighs over 300 pounds, we understood that this little event could quickly turn into a very serious situation. This is not to mention the fact that actually ten people currently stayed in the house, six of them adolescents, who would at some point also need to use the facilities.

But, as luck would have it, Pete worked as a pipe fitter, and as such was a pretty handy guy where plumbing is concerned. Robert and Pete proceeded to the basement to save the day. Pete believed that, with just a few tools (supplied by Uncle Dale, who dropped them off and then ran like hell, which proved to be very insightful), he could fix the problem in no time.

I can't tell you precisely what happened next, as Tara and I continued chatting endlessly at the kitchen table while the guys toiled in the basement. What I can tell you is that about an hour later when Tara and I went to assess the situation, Pete looked like something out of the movie *Ghost*. You remember the scene with the pottery wheel, and Demi Moore and Patrick Swaze ended up covered in mud? That's what Pete resembled, except I can assure you that it wasn't mud he was covered with. Robert kept his distance as much as possible, and his skin tone resembled something close to the color of the *Grinch*. Pete acted none too happy, either, and I am a direct witness to the fact that it did smell pretty rank down there. Despite it all, Pete persisted and finally cleaned out the pipes, and the facilities worked once again. He took an hour-long shower afterwards and managed to use up all the hot water, but no one complained as we all agreed he deserved it. He was definitely the man of the hour, and as such Tara and I let the guys win at cards that night. But don't tell them. We wouldn't want them to think that we had enough compassion to actually throw a serious game of cards.

The stay at Grandma Nola's house turned out to be a memorable experience. My two boys, Eric and Jess, and Tara and Pete's clan, Tiffany, Heidi, Devon, and Wayne all managed to put up with each other. I guess the fact of the mix, three boys and three girls, helped. And, of course, it doesn't hurt that we don't have to put up with each other very often. Seeing the family again, aunts and uncles, cousins and grandparents, felt great as well. It makes me thankful every day that my Dad took us far enough away to only have to visit occasionally! Just kidding. I love them all and feel lucky to have each and every one of them at least 500 miles away!

What Kind of Head?

In the interest of clarity, I begin with a story about Tara's fondness for a particular vacation spot before moving on to our vacations together. It seems that Tara can't get enough of a good thing—or maybe it's that she refuses to admit defeat. Regardless, she is drawn to a small expanse of land on the North Carolina coast. Frankly, I am puzzled as to the root cause of her fascination with this area. I force myself to believe her desire to travel to the area must be based on more than empirical evidence, because her past experiences have been less than rewarding. Although, once again, I must also consider the possibility that she is a complete lunatic.

Some years ago, Tara and her girlfriends decided that they needed an excuse to get together, without the men in their lives. In order to accomplish this feat, they decided to form a women's club. The idea of the club was to create a nifty arrangement for the women: each month they pay a predetermined amount into a due's bucket, and, by the end of the year, they have collected enough to fund a seven-day vacation for the entire group. I don't know if they lack inspiration or if they just love the beach above all else, but every year they end up renting a beach house at Nags Head, North Carolina and spend a week together. The money that they put in the kitty for their dues pre-pays for the weekly rental of the house. Other than that, everyone is expected to take additional cash for their food and any other essentials for the week.

The general area in which Nags Head is located is called the Outer Banks. The reason that it's called the Outer Banks is because there are actually two shorelines. The Outer Banks is a one-mile-wide piece of land that runs parallel to the mainland shoreline for several miles. Water separates the mainland and the island, which is perhaps more accurately described as a sandbar sitting above the water. The mainland is called the Inner Banks, in contrast to the mini-island Outer Banks. The only land passages to the Outer Banks are a couple of lengthy bridges that span the water separating the mainland from this island. Trust me, this information will prove relevant.

One particular year, Tara and her friends arrived on Saturday at the beach house, marking an uneventful start to their excursion. The drill repeats the same every year: unpack, make a list of necessities, go to the store, and then hit the beach. One of the girls always brings a blender for frozen margaritas, daiquiris, Pina coladas, and other beach-appropriate drinks that can only be improved upon by the addition of a shiny foil umbrella. Most of the women bring their own alcohol, so they don't have to pay an exorbitant price for it at a popular tourist locale. Usually, the only items they have to pick up at the store are food and mixers (or, in descending order of importance, mixers and food).

After they finished unpacking that year, they went to the store to collect their essentials. After returning to the house and concocting a pitcher of frozen drinks to take with them, they headed for the beach. The rental house sat adjacent to the beach, so they didn't have far to walk to find a worthy spot for their beach towels. All the girls got settled and each procured her share of the pitcher of frozen drinks. Tara prefers an insulated mug to a paper cup, because the drink stays frozen longer. She filled her mug and sat on the beach, basking in the sun and loving life.

It seemed to Tara that afternoon that the waves appeared to be particularly lively, but she didn't really think too much about it; sometimes the ocean just is more active than at other times. Debra, one of the members of the club, swam out in the waves and played in the surf. She swam in far enough that her whole body became submerged, except for her head. She bounced up and down impishly, yelling for the other girls to join her and frolic in the surf with her. A couple of the other women, probably just wanting to shut Debra up, began walking towards the water (Tara was too smart for that ploy; besides, she had a frozen drink to attend to). Of course, when ocean water first hits you, it feels extremely cold. But once you get used to it, it seems like it's not so frigid. Debra must've been particularly warm-blooded, because the other two women had a difficult time convincing themselves to plunge their scantily clad bodies into the cold water. As they approached the frigid water, the waves rushed towards them and they shrieked and retreated a safe distance from the pounding surf. Debra became agitated with them and called them sissies. She taunted their cowardice as they danced along the beach in an effort to escape the algid surf.

One of the retreating girls turned back towards Debra, ready to spout an unoriginal response (not fit for prime-time audiences) to Debra's haranguing. But instead, her eyes snapped widely open and she began to yell, "Debra, run! Swim! Get out of there!" Debra immediately became puzzled by her friend's concerned response so she spun around in the water, looking across the vast immensity of the ocean to see a colossal wave racing towards her.

Debra attempted to move quickly in the water, but you know how the feeling of trepidation consumes you and you just can't seem to move fast enough? She tried to run but the weight of the water burdened her stride. She then decided to swim for her life. When she reached a spot that was shallow and the water hit her below the waist, she ran for it. Her legs reached and stretched, as each foot surfaced above the ocean water and quickly disappeared back into the water at a spot a few feet closer to safety. Tara said she had never seen Debra move so fast. About the time she almost reached a safe haven, the wave hit her square in the back. Instantaneously, her neck snapped back as her spine arched against the pressure of her adversary. Seconds later, the wave swallowed her up.

The other women couldn't see her for a few seconds, and then she suddenly appeared about ten feet up the beach. She had done a face plant into the sand. As she rose, shaken and startled, but okay, she began articulating her experience. She exclaimed, "Wow, what a wave! Did you guys see that? I thought I was done for!" Her excitement about the experience obviously overcame the pain of her lacerated body. "I mean, seriously, guys," Debra gesticulated wildly, "I've never *seen* a wave that big!" The girls tried to keep straight faces; after all, Debra had come close to getting gravely injured, but they just couldn't manage it after a few seconds. Debra creased her brows. "What?! What's so darn funny?" Then, she looked down and realized her bathing suit top was nowhere to be seen. Of course, when she realized she didn't have a top on, she dove for her towel on the sand about fifteen feet away. Tara and the other girls got quite a kick out of watching Debra relay her harrowing experience sans bathing suit top . . . along with all the other tourists on the beach. Needless to say, it was back to the store, since Debra had to buy a new bathing suit—or at least a new top.

That evening, the girls sat around and visited with each other, looking forward to their week at the beach. Tara sat up with some of them until late, playing games and enjoying her leisure time. They took pleasure in each other's company until the wee hours of the morning. Then Tara and the other die-hards hit the sack.

The next morning, despite the late night, Tara arose bright and early. Before any of the other girls got up, the phone rang. She answered it and it was one of the other women's husbands. He asked, "What are you girls doing?" Tara told him that they weren't doing anything yet, that everyone else was still in bed. He said, "Aren't they evacuating the Outer Banks?" Tara inquired as to what he meant and he told her to turn on the television. That was the first time on the trip that the television or radio had been on, and the women were not aware that a hurricane quickly approached the area. She bore the name of Emily, and she planned a vicious strike. The husband on the phone sounded distressed, telling Tara that they all needed to distance themselves from the coast. She told him that she would convene with the others and they would let him know what they decided to do.

Of course, first thing in the morning when the women get up, there is really only one thing on their minds: breakfast! Everyone has priorities, and for the women's club, food was first and foremost (well, in the mornings it was; alcohol had top billing most other times of the day). Of course, due to the amount of alcohol they consumed on their weeklong excursions, they had to have large quantities food to remain lucid. After all the other women sprang from their bunks, they decided that the needed discussion could occur over breakfast. They piled into their cars and headed down the road to the nearest restaurant. Uncertain as to what solution they would reach, everyone took their essentials. Tara had her purse and an overnight bag, and the other women had similar bags in tow. Before they pulled out of the driveway, though, Robin started yelling, "Wait! I forgot something." She ran back into the house and a few minutes later she emerged carrying the blender. I guess that was a priority for her, and I assure you the rest of the group appreciated her thoughtfulness.

While they relaxed at the restaurant and ate breakfast, everyone talked about Emily. The local residents weren't being forced to evacuate, but according to the waitress at the restaurant, all the tourists had to leave the Outer Banks. As the women finished their meals, they all decided that the best course of action was to head west, away from the coast. They finished eating and, after paying the bill, they again piled into their vehicles. Robin, who had felt compelled to return to the house before breakfast to get the blender, realized that she didn't have her purse with her. I guess she had a one-track mind with the blender and all. As a result, one of the vehicles had to drive back to the house so that Robin could retrieve her purse before they left the island.

The rest of the women stood around by the other cars, chatting about where they should go and how to find accommodations once they got there. Several little towns were scattered across the countryside, all within an hour's drive, so Shelly, who was Miss Organized, commandeered a phone book and started calling hotels in the neighboring towns only to discover that the rest of the vacationers had kept up with the local news and many of them had already left that morning or the night before. Every hotel, motel, or bed and breakfast that Shelly called was booked full. No vacancies existed in any town within an hour's drive.

By the time Shelly had called all the hotels in the phone book, the other car had returned. Robin sat in the back seat, grasping her purse in one arm and the blender in the other, as if she could already sense the pull of the hurricane's winds. The girls decided they would travel west while Shelly would continue to call various places of lodging as they drove. The route had been set, so Shelly had the job of investigating the upcoming areas as they drove and call every hotel in their path before they reached it.

A few of the women started making noise about going home. Tara decidedly didn't like that turn of events. She kept saying, "This is *our* week and we are *not* going home. We can find a nice place to stay and still have a good time. Besides, we'll be back at the beach within a few days, so let's just go and have a good time." They all finally agreed that it would be an adventure, so they climbed into the cars and headed west.

As they drove, Shelly canvassed every hotel in the area all to no avail; absolutely no vacancies existed. Each time she completed a call, she crossed out the hotel on the list to ensure she didn't duplicate her efforts. Her mission was clear: find a place, any place, for them to stay. She wasn't having any luck locating a hotel within two hours of the coast. She began searching for an appropriate hotel in the next town out, Tarboro. I think that human nature is to stick with what is familiar to you, so she began by contacting the hotel and motel names that she recognized, like Holiday Inn and Motel 6. It quickly became deja vu. All the rooms were full; absolutely no vacancies existed anywhere. Shelly then continued through the list of names that sounded unfamiliar to her, and her first choice was the Tarboro Inn. She felt the word "Inn" had a quaint, warm feel to it, and therefore, she picked that one first. When she called them, they said— miraculously—that they had vacancies, so Shelly booked a couple of rooms for the girls to stay in that night.

Everyone felt relieved that they didn't have to drive any further than Tarboro. They had already ventured a few hours off the coast, and they didn't want to end up in the next state to find accommodations. Tara tried to stay upbeat and talked about what a great adventure they'd had so far. The effect was contagious; even the girls who had become grumpy earlier began to lighten up and have a good time. Shelly received directions from the hotel clerk on how to get to the Tarboro Inn once they arrived in town, and with no trouble at all, they drove right to it. To their surprise, the parking lot appeared to be very sparsely populated.

They stopped the car and peered up at the hotel. The exterior of the hotel appeared unkempt, with several of the windows shattered. Although the sign out front read "Great Rates, Pool, and Air Conditioning," the hotel's appearance suggested none of these amenities. The women looked at each other, bewildered and uncertain as to what they should do. Shelly grabbed the phone and started calling all the other hotels in the area, but with no success. Tara continued to rally the group and rambled on, expressing her optimism, "Hey, look. It'll be fun. We always have a good time. They've got air conditioning and a pool. I bet they even have beds to sleep on. And let's face it; it's better than sleeping in the car." I'm actually surprised that one of the other ladies didn't haul off and belt her for her relentless optimism in the face of certain doom. Instead, they just looked at her and said, "Fine, but only if we get a room with a window that isn't broken."

They entered the hotel in search of room assignments. The clerk at the front desk appeared to be Indian and didn't speak clear English. The women muddled through the conversation and managed to secure rooms without broken windows, although the rooms still left a lot to be desired. The musty smell of the draperies and the muted appearance of the cloth surfaces made the rooms unappealing. Still, they tried to see the bright side and thought, what the heck, at least the bed linens appeared to be laundered. After settling into their rooms, they decided to go into town and get something to eat (it's a familiar theme). As they drove into town, they passed a couple of other hotels that were obviously full, since their parking lots were cluttered with cars and motor homes. They remained slightly puzzled by the fact that the parking lot at their hotel had only a smattering of vehicles in it—although not the nicest place, but appeared to be habitable—but they assumed that many people had called ahead, made reservations, and not yet arrived.

When they arrived at the restaurant, they grabbed a table and sat down. The restaurant was packed, most probably with tourists who had also been diverted west. A waitress walked up to the table, handed everyone a menu and asked to get their drink order. Tara, who is also Miss Curiosity, said, "Are you guys always this busy, or are these people from the coast, trying to put some distance between them and the hurricane?" The waitress said, yes, that most of the customers were tourists trying to escape Emily's path and then asked the women where they were staying. Tara said that they had booked at the Tarboro Inn. The waitress gasped and said, "You all aren't really staying there, are you?" Tara said, "Yes, why? What's wrong?" For the first time that day, even Tara's face fell a bit at the shock in the waitress's voice. The waitress proceeded to tell them that the Tarboro Inn was where all the drug dealers and the prostitutes did their business. She said it was Tarboro's "rooms by the hour" establishment.

Some of the women became instantly mortified. Tara looked around the room, running a worried hand through her hair, and made a perhaps insane decision to become amused by the whole incident. She smiled weakly and said, "Oh boy. What an adventure!" Obviously, the others contemplated the situation from quite different points of view, wondering if their near future included a life-threatening event. That started the grumbling all over again and the debate ensued as to whether or not they should head towards home. Tara felt determined not to let anyone go home, because she feared that, if they went home, they would end up staying there the rest of the week and throw away their vacation money that they put down on the beach-front property. She started to lobby hard for them to at least stay the night and see what the weather forecast predicted for the next day. Finally, although it was pretty apparent they didn't want to, all the girls decided to stay for the night. Tara immediately began thinking hard about how to convince them to stay the next day while the rest of them concentrated on how early they could get the heck out of Tarboro.

After they finished eating and returned to the hotel, they decided the time had come for some frozen adult beverages. Robin, the Keeper of the Blender, found a convenient spot to plug it in. After adding all the necessary ingredients and pushing the Puree button, a circuit blew and all the lights went out except for the one in the main room. Tara didn't seem to think that this presented a lasting problem, so she called the front desk and told the clerk what happened. She assumed that they would just reset the breakers and the electricity would be available again. When the Indian man arrived at their door with a plunger, Tara knew something had gotten lost in the communication of the event. Due to this lack of understanding, she figured they didn't really need more than one operable circuit and they would just have to deal with it while they stayed there. Since the electricity remained intact in the main room, the women moved their supplies to that area and proceeded to imbibe.

During the night, all kinds of commotion rang throughout the hotel. People noisily walked up and down the stairs, and loud voices emanated from the corridor. Of course, none of the women had the guts (or maybe I should say stupidity) to open their door and see what was going on. They assumed that it was business as usual for that establishment, and if the waitress's suspicions held true, then this hotel's busiest time of the day would be after the sun had set. Apparently, by the sound of it, a very *long* time after the sun had set.

The next morning the girls got up and went to breakfast, despite not being very well-rested. When they glanced out of the thankfully paned window, they saw that the previously empty parking lot was full of motor homes, station wagons and mini vans. It looked like the rest of the evacuators had found the Tarboro Inn for a night. Even a glass truck sat in the parking lot and a couple of guys worked busily replacing broken windows. Seemed the Tarboro Inn made enough money in one night to fix the place up a little bit. The news reports came in optimistically about everyone being able to return to the coast the following day, so Tara lobbied hard for everyone to stay and return to Nags Head the following morning. Most of the girls agreed, but a few of them had had it with the lack of sleep and uncertainty, so they decided that they were just going to head home. The rest of them returned to the hotel with the intention of lounging around the pool for the afternoon.

The women put on their swimsuits and proceeded downstairs. Tara noticed a sign with an arrow that said "Pool Area," so they followed the sign to the back of the hotel. When they opened the door, they noticed the area hadn't been well maintained (now, there's a shocker) and the decking area was cracked with weeds protruding through the breaks in the cement. Tara pretended not to notice and said, "Well, it's a little rundown, but who cares. We'll have fun." After they walked down some stairs and around some overgrown shrubs, the pool was in full sight of the women. It was a pretty good size pool, which was nice—however, there was only about a foot of water in the bottom. The green water had algae and disgusting slime floating on top of the stagnant water. Tara walked over to one of the lounge chairs, noticing it contained no fabric or cushions to sit on. Merely a metal frame existed in place of what used to be a chaise lounge chair. She placed her towel inside the metal frame and, after climbing into the center, lie down on the cement and proceeded to sunbathe.

The other women shook their heads in disbelief, but if you've ever had one of those days where everything went awry, you understand that, beyond a certain point, calamities become hilarious. I think it is the mind's way of protecting your brain from exploding. From that moment on, everyone started giggling and acting silly. They even took some group pictures. They all lined up in their bathing suits and sat with their legs hanging over the edge of the nearly empty pool. One of the attendants in the hotel took their pictures. They pretended to be lounging at a luxurious hotel and having a great time. The truth of the matter was that they did have a great time from that moment forward. They decided that they were going to have a good time regardless of the surroundings. After all, they had the pool all to themselves.

The next morning they headed back to the coast, as Emily had left the area, and they were all delighted to find their beach house still intact. The rest of the week's activities occurred uneventfully, while the friends enjoyed the sun, sand, and surf. Even today, when they discuss their trips, their venture to Tarboro always seems to come up. It seems that when things don't go as planned, the memories are more vivid and shine brighter than when they do.

A Bunch of Hot Air

As the years passed, Tara and I realized that we hadn't spent sufficient time together as a family. So, we decided to make a commitment to have our two families meet at least once a year. The first year was 1994. Tara said she knew a great stretch of beach in North Carolina on the Outer Banks called Nags Head. At the time, I had not heard about Nags Head and thought the name was quite unusual; it sounded like trouble to me. Little did I know. Of course, Tara hadn't shared the story of her previous excursion until we had already arrived.

Robert, the boys, and I lived in Oklahoma at the time (yes, we had moved yet again). I worked for a major airline and, although we could fly inexpensively, we decided to drive so we could see the countryside firsthand. Robert and the boys had never been east of the Mississippi River. Believe it or not, I actually prefer driving to flying. Most people think I am insane, but I rationalize it as a control issue. When you fly, you have absolutely no control over your arrival time—or, for that matter, what city you end up in, or if your luggage makes it with you, and so on. We calculated that the road trip would take about 20 hours, but culturally speaking, we would be fulfilled by the time we arrived on the coast. In my mind, I thought the drive would be much more enriching than spending the day at 30,000 feet and inside airport terminals.

We decided to leave Oklahoma at around 4:00 p.m. on Friday and planned to drive until we grew tired, at which time we would stop and spend the night. We thought we could cover at least half the distance the first day and be able to arrive in Nags Head around dinnertime on Saturday. We formulated a plan. Follow Interstate 40 through Arkansas and Tennessee, then pull over and spend the night. The next morning we could traverse the Smokey Mountains. I truly believed the boys would enjoy the scenery and I wanted them to experience the difference in geography of the various areas in the United States. They had spent most of their life west of the Rocky Mountains, so I thought it would be nice for them to see another example of Mother Nature's pinnacles.

As we approached Knoxville, Tennessee, Robert and I became extremely tired. The clock approached 2:00 a.m. and Robert said that he just couldn't drive any farther. I found this slightly amusing since all night I kept saying, "Why don't you let me drive for a while so you can rest." But he wouldn't relinquish the wheel. I figured out at that point the two worst fears of men: the first involves stopping to ask for directions (directophobia, or something like that). The second fear is letting your wife drive while you sleep (femaledriverphobia). Anyway, by that time, I felt pretty fatigued as well, so I suggested we find a cheap motel and catch a few hours sleep. We stopped on the outskirts of Kingston, Tennessee. I thought it looked like a great spot, since neon signs lit up the blackened sky.

Have you ever noticed that, when there is space available, you can see the "vacancy" signs for miles, but when the motels are full, the "no vacancy" signs are nowhere to be seen? So, no surprise here: there were no rooms available. I told Robert at the last motel, "Well, let's just drive up the road a bit and get a room." The man behind the counter (I can't really tell you what I called him) said, "Y'all won't find a room within a couple hundernt miles a' here." I said "Why not?" He responded, "Well ma'am, it is Fourth of July weekend." I'm thinking, "SO!! Like people don't travel without any reservations on one of the busiest holiday weekends of the year?" I felt pretty stupid about that time, and nothing pisses me off more than stupidity, especially when it's my own. You know when you get pissed off and the adrenaline starts flowing and you're just not tired anymore? Those emotions described my demeanor that night. As I climbed behind the wheel, I told Robert to shut up and go to sleep. Next thing I knew I drove into the Smokey Mountains as the three men in my life slept like babies.

The Smokey Mountains are named as such for a very good reason; let me enlighten you. As the men in my life slept without a care in the world, I started climbing the mountain roads in the mini-van. The higher I drove, the foggier it became. As I continued my ascent, signs dotted the side of the road that read, "15 miles per hour when flashing." Highly concerned, I thought, if those damned lights started flashing, we wouldn't get to Nags Head until the end of the week! Luckily, a person in a small car passed me and appeared to know her way through the mountains, so I followed her through the fog. I stayed close enough behind her to extend my field of vision, but far enough back to easily anticipate the curves in the road. Once we reached the summit and the road began its downward slope, I felt relieved that we were literally on the downhill side. As we descended back to sea level on the other side of the mountains around Asheville, North Carolina, the men in my life began to stir. Thankfully, the sun dawned on the horizon and the fog had lifted (or at least we sat underneath it). Oh, and here's a news flash for you: immediately upon waking, the guys felt hungry.

After driving all night while Robert slept, I knew he would be eager to regain control of the wheel. Once he was conscious, the femaledriverphobia had started to set in again. So, after stopping for gas and a bite to eat, Robert regained what he felt was his rightful place behind the wheel, and we arrived in Nags Head just shortly after noon. As we drove up to the house, we noticed that it consisted of a wood frame and sat on stilts. Although not much to look, it seemed to be comparable to the other rentals in the vicinity. As we drove up to the house and parked, my oldest son, Eric, exclaimed, "Oh, great! It's Chevy Chase's Summer Vacation!" I never thought of Eric being even slightly clairvoyant, but at the time I assumed his reference related to the unimpressive rental house in which we were about to spend a week. In retrospect, knowing that when the Griswolds take to the road, its one unexpected event after another, most of them unpleasant I might add, I think he may have a knack at foreseeing future events. Tara and Pete stood outside, busily unpacking their car. Tara turned to me and said, "You're early!" I gave her a go-to-hell look and that was enough communication between sisters. She knows when to let things slide.

The next morning after some much-needed sleep, we ran down to the local convenience market and stocked the coolers full of ice to keep the beer and wine cold. Then, we hit the beach. Last time we were together in Indiana, you would have appropriately been able to use the cliché "when hell freezes over." This time it was like hell as we all fear it—heat like I'd never experienced, and the humidity was fierce! Every time you took a breath, you had to swallow. But compared to the night before, I enjoyed the hell out of it. That night, we went out for an all-you-can-eat seafood buffet. We spent three hours there, a half hour waiting to be seated and two and a half hours stuffing our faces. We love the coast!

I arose slightly sluggish the next morning. Getting no sleep two nights before had finally caught up with me. It felt hot and humid, and I woke up with my legs stuck together. After we got a bite to eat, we hit the beach again for some rest and relaxation. The temperature was blistering, but I still enjoyed the idle time. I fell asleep in the sun, and when I awoke, my right ear, which had been facing the sun, was plugged up. I literally couldn't hear out of it. So, Tara and I went back to the house and attempted unplugging my ear using baby oil and peroxide, but neither worked. I knew that a large piece of wax obstructed my ear canal, since I had the waxiest ears of anyone I knew. Thus, I remained confident that it wasn't a life-threatening condition and decided that I could ignore it until we returned home the following weekend. Until then, my attention stayed focused on more immediately pressing issues, like the unbearable heat.

It seemed as if the temperature continued to rise in the house. Everyone sweated profusely and it began smelling a little ripe in the small rental house. Pete, all 300+ pounds of him, looked as if he felt poorly. We soon realized that the air conditioner had quit. Tara said, "No problem, I'll just call maintenance and they'll come out and fix it." She called and they told her not to fret. They said for us to go out to dinner and, when we returned, the air would be cool. We decided to hit the seafood buffet again. Scallops, shrimp, crab, all you could eat—and, believe me, our crew could eat a lot. Needless to say, I think we got our money's worth. Life was good! We returned to the rental house, full and sleepy. It still felt very warm inside, but we crashed anyway, with no clothes or covers on. The humidity was a killer.

The next morning I woke up drenched. I knew it was time for a cold shower to cool down the old body. By the time I got out of the shower, I felt refreshed. We ran down the street to the market for ice to re-stock the coolers. We might be able to withstand the heat ourselves, but we certainly couldn't allow the beer and wine to get warm. We hit the beach for a little sun (and I mean a little, since we had been sweating for two days straight), and then we returned to the house. We quickly realized the air conditioner was still inoperable. Pete's face bore a deep shade of red. He fanned himself while sitting at the kitchen table. Tara and I became increasingly concerned, as Pete is a big guy and outwardly showed obvious signs of distress. While Robert called maintenance to see what the status of our repair was, Tara and I put Pete in the bathtub and dumped the contents of the cooler on him, ice, beer and all. He immediately responded with a smile. He felt like one cool dude and didn't even have to get up to fetch himself a beer.

In the meantime, we all took turns showering in the other bathroom. One thing was for certain: we didn't have to worry about running out of hot water because we weren't using any. The heat remained unbearable. We showered about three times a day just to stay cool. My ear was still plugged, but it didn't hurt so I still didn't become concerned. I just couldn't hear out of it, which irritated me but didn't necessarily cause me any undue distress. There was still no sign of maintenance. Although the rest of us started feeling nauseous from the heat, Pete felt great (and I don't think it was from the ice bath!).

The next morning I woke up in a sweat, which felt like life as usual by that time. I took a shower and discovered that I ran seriously low on clean underwear. Time to gather the dirty clothes and proceed with laundry duties. Tara and I searched the house for everyone's soiled clothing and we ended up with an entire load of white underwear. An hour later, after the washer finished its cycle, we threw the underwear in the dryer. Although the house remained unbearably hot, we knew that we had to have clean underwear. After about 30 minutes, Tara got up and checked the clothes in the dryer. The underwear felt damp, which we thought was odd, since it usually doesn't take very long to dry underwear. We knew that different appliances performed differently, so we assumed, since we were unfamiliar with that particular dryer, that maybe it took longer to dry underwear than the dryers we had at home. After the dryer shut off at the end of its second cycle, the underwear still felt wet. Tara and I looked at one another and suddenly it dawned on us: the heating element in the dryer didn't work. Although the clothes tumbled around and around, they were not drying. Tara and I quickly derived a solution. We tied a rope on each end of the porch and fashioned a clothesline. Then we hung the panties and boxers out to dry, for the whole world to see. We thought our ingenuity had outdone itself that day, but trying to line-dry clothes in 99+% humidity is an exercise of sheer futility. Here's some advice: don't bother because it doesn't work!

Over those few days, frustration slowly became our dominant emotion. We had changed clothes so many times we dirtied every pair of clean underwear again (except for Pete who still sat in the bathtub singing 100 bottles of beer on the wall; I was surprised he could still count). The air conditioning remained inoperable so we sweated our asses off, and the dryer didn't work, so we didn't have any clean clothes (well, clean maybe, but not clean and *dry*). And my ear was still plugged. About as far from being a happy camper than I could possibly imagine, I knew the only thing that could raise my spirits was to share my grief with someone I didn't care much about (okay, so maybe someone I had come to despise). Therefore, I volunteered to call maintenance since my frame of mind was in the perfect temperament to give them a little piece of it (not that I have that much to spare). Ultimatum time had arrived. I told them to fix the air (and now the dryer too), or we were departing, expecting a full refund for the entire week. We decided to go out to dinner for seafood again. It quickly became apparent that we started spending more time at the restaurant than in the rental house. The restaurant's air conditioning offered comfort and pleasure to our over-heated, miserable bodies, so we spent hours gorging ourselves with shellfish. When we returned to the rental house about four hours later, two of the three bedrooms had window air conditioning units in them. They ran full blast, distributing cool, dry air throughout the two rooms. I thought I had a near-death experience, as I have never been so close to heaven in my life. The biggest challenge was how to fit eight people into two small bedrooms, but we didn't complain at that point.

The next day was our last full day in Nags Head. I woke up loving life, since, for the first time since we'd been there, my thighs weren't stuck together. In fact, I realized I felt frozen, but I didn't dare turn off the air conditioning. A sense of fear lurked in the back of my mind that, if I dared to turn off the air conditioner, when I attempted turn it back on, it wouldn't start. (Paranoia clearly crept in: I heard a faint little voice in the back of my head taunting me, "Yeah, go ahead and turn it off, and see what happens when you can't get it started again! They'll be a lynching!") Anyway, Tara and I hit the beach for one last time that week. My ear was still plugged, but I just continued to ignored it. Our time at the beach had slowly disintegrated to about 15 minutes at a time because of the heat and the sand. But it's the principle of the situation. When you are at the beach, you must go to the beach and lie out. But, frankly, it just didn't feel that enjoyable anymore. Tara and I decided that we felt pretty burnt out on the sun and the sand, so we went back to the beach house. We decided to eat in that night, since the temperature in the house had improved greatly. Guess what was on the menu? We went down the street to a seafood market and got some fresh shrimp, scallops, clams, and crab legs— enough for yet another feast. We steamed it all, and it tasted delicious, just as good as the seafood buffets. Afterwards, the time had arrived for our nightly game of cards. Euchre was the chosen game for the evening and the battle of the sexes, guys against the gals, ensued.

But just as the game got underway, Tara started itching and scratching her thighs and arms. I looked over at her and observed that her skin had broken out in hives. We ran to the store and picked up some Benadryl. Apparently, Tara has a weird allergic reaction to eating an over-abundance of crabmeat. The strange thing is that she can eat crab without it bothering her; she just can't eat it every night for a week. She took the Benadryl and quickly became drowsy. I yelled at her, "Don't fall asleep, man! I can't beat these guys by myself!" Then she started to lose her voice. I thought, oh, great! I can't hear and now Tara's voice was down to a whisper. She said something to me and I yelled back, "WHAT?!!" She wrote on a piece of paper, "I can hear, ding-dong; I just can't talk." So, I yelled back again, "OKAY!" She pointed to the paper and wrote, "You don't have to yell; I can hear just fine." "Oh, sorry," I said, in what I hoped was a more normal tone of voice. Communication definitely fell short on the gal's team that night.

The next morning we arose fairly early to get a head start on our twenty-hour road excursion. The worst part about driving across country on vacation is the trip home. Now that we had seen it all before it just wasn't as interesting—at least to me. Of course, Robert and the boys didn't act bored, as they had slept all the way through the last part of the trip coming to Nags Head. Oh, how I wished I could sleep in a car.

Anyway, the trip home occurred uneventfully, and we all had a great time. The day after we got home, I went to the doctor and he removed the wax plug from my right ear. It sounded very strange, but comforting, hearing in stereo again. I heard that Tara got her voice back as well. It was a good thing or else our phone conversations would have posed a real challenge in the days ahead.

A Dog's Tail (or Two)

When Robert and I were first married, Robert worked as a forklift driver at an appliance warehouse. Robert had made a few friends at the plant, and one day decided to invite one of his new friends, Hank, and his wife to dinner. Knowing what an animal lover I was, Robert asked them to bring their dog with them. He was just a puppy, half St. Bernard, half Samoyed, and they named him Ben. Ben and I fell in love at once and, when Hank saw me and Ben playing together, he offered to give us Ben. Hank and Bonnie were about to have their first child and felt concerned that they would not be able to give Ben the attention that he deserved. Of course, one glance at the joy on my face convinced Robert it would be for the best if we accepted Ben into our home.

Robert and I lived in a one-bedroom apartment at the time, so there wasn't a lot of available space. Ben was just a puppy, though, and we felt happy to be a close-knit family. Hank and Bonnie failed to tell us, however, that Ben had an apparent underwear fetish. Coupled with the fact that Robert had a bad habit of leaving his boxer shorts lying on the bedroom floor, Ben followed his quest in life and chewed the crotch out of every pair of boxer shorts that Robert owned. Needless to say, Robert and I spent a lot of time and money keeping him in underwear during that time. You would think that Robert would simply quit leaving his undergarments all over the floor, but I guess the saying "you can't teach an old dog new tricks" didn't necessarily apply only to our canine friends.

While I don't really like stories with sad endings, my stories would just not be complete without sharing all of my memories of Ben. When we acquired Ben, he had distemper, although he didn't show any signs of the disease at that time. After about the first week that we had him, though, he developed a bad case of diarrhea. We had to lock him in the bathroom area when we went to work, since the tiled floor was easy to clean up. Although not an ideal solution, we couldn't simply skip work to care for a sick dog.

When Robert arrived home one day and opened the door to the bathroom, there was an unexpectedly horrific mess. Robert had left his blow dryer on the vanity, and Ben succeeded in getting it down and managed to wrap it around his neck. He almost chewed through the electrical cord, which would have been a shocking experience for him, since the blow dryer remained plugged in. But, Ben just stood there, obliviously wagging his tail, with that blow dryer swinging from side to side around his neck. Of course, he had also managed to drag the blow dryer all over the bathroom, and it was caked with . . . well, as mentioned, Ben was sick, so I will let you figure it out. It took Robert hours to clean the blow dryer completely, using an old toothbrush and toothpicks to get in between all the hot air vent openings on it.

A few days later when I came home, Robert told me that Ben was sleeping, but not in the comforts of our home. Although the truth was left unspoken, I knew what he meant. Robert knew that I would not consent to ending Ben's life, although he watched my daily pain as Ben's condition deteriorated. I knew that our precious time with Ben had come to an end. I knew in my heart that now he must be with Quacky, chasing cars and being carefree. Even though Ben never had the pleasure of pursuing that activity during his short time on earth, I knew that Quacky, being the master car-chaser, would find pleasure in teaching the young pup the rules of the road. And I think that Ben could teach Quacky a thing or two about underwear.

Tara has also had her share of heart-breaking loses with her canine companions, one of them in particular, Tommy, who may not have been flawless, but was perfect in Tara's eyes. Tommy, a Springer Spaniel, came from a litter that a friend of Tara's had been blessed with from her own female Springer Spaniel. Named the pick of the litter, Tommy bore the label of "show-quality." Initially excited about having a pup of such high quality, Tara's friend spoke highly of her newest arrival; that is, until she discovered that he only had one testicle. Since that is considered a breeding defect, he couldn't participate in dog shows. Tara's friend neutered him and asked Tara if she would like to have him. She knew that Tara would give him a good home, and so Tara agreed to take him, and the two quickly became constant companions.

Tommy enjoyed going for rides in Tara's truck. She wouldn't allow him to ride in the bed, but instead Tommy sat next to her in the front seat. When they traveled for quite a distance, Tara would roll down Tommy's window so he could hang his head out and enjoy the fresh air. His long, floppy ears flapped back and forth with the wind and his gums folded down from the force of the pressure. When he opened his mouth, revealing his pleasure, the wind became trapped inside his mouth and blew up his cheeks like balloons. When they reached their destination, the hair on Tommy's head would be plastered straight back from the force of the wind, so Tara would grab Tommy's head and muss up his facial fur, returning it to its normal ad hoc stance.

Tommy loved being inside the house with the family. Tara let him in frequently, since he minded his manners, even while the family enjoyed their evening meal together. Tommy would lie quietly beside the dinner table, never begging, but always keeping one eye open, waiting patiently to clean up the leftovers that Tara always shared with him. Tommy and Tara became inseparable while Tara was at home, and as such, they became best friends.

Unfortunately, Springer Spaniels only have a life expectancy of about twelve years, so after Tommy passed his eleventh year, Tara knew his time on this earth was becoming short. He had developed cataracts, and thus didn't see very well, and his hearing had also failed. Through most of his life, whenever Tara returned home from work, Tommy would bark when he heard her truck coming up the road. As he got older, sometimes he wouldn't wake up until after she was already parked and out of the truck. So, Tara took to tiptoeing up to him, patting him gently on the side and murmuring, "I snuck up on you, Tommy." Tommy would wake up immediately and wag his tail, oblivious to his own failing health, then accompany Tara to the pasture for the horses' nightly feeding.

One night when Tara got home from the bowling alley, Tommy lay in the backyard on his side. She walked over to him and, as she reached down to pat him on his side, she realized that he had died. She went on to the pasture to feed the horses, her eyes a little moist; she knew that Pete followed closely behind her and would discover Tommy's dead body. She felt prepared to deal with her dog's death, as she had been anticipating his passing, but didn't want to attempt moving him alone. When Pete drove in a few minutes later, he called out, "Hey, Tara. I think Tommy's dead." She sighed and responded, "Yeah, I know. Would you please take care of it?"

Pete went into the house and came back out with a garbage bag. He placed Tommy's body in the bag, put him in the wheelbarrow and wheeled him to the back of the yard beside the shed. Since it was late and Pete had to work the next day, he called his son Wayne, who wasn't working at the time and asked him if he would come up and bury Tommy the next day. Even though the air was frigid since half of the month of November had already passed, Wayne agreed and Pete described to him where to bury Tommy.

When Wayne arrived at the house the next day and walked out into the backyard, he found Sundance, Pete's yellow Labrador, in the wheelbarrow lying on top of Tommy's bagged body. In addition, Noah, Tara's Great Pyrenees, lay under the wheelbarrow just below Tommy's body. It appeared as if they wanted to keep Tommy from being taken away. Wayne shook his head, ignoring the dogs' concern out of necessity, and started digging. The frozen ground, nearly as hard as rock, initially seemed impenetrable, but eventually Wayne managed to dig a hole big enough in which to put Tommy's body and cover it up. But when he took Tommy out of the wheelbarrow and placed him in the hole, Noah and Sundance started barking. They began with low, guttural growls that rose into a full-fledged howling ballad, as if to pay tribute to their friend and prevent his burial. Wayne felt a bit shaken by such a display, though he knew the chore had to be done, so he finished filling the hole with loose dirt, completing the task by packing the dirt down with the shovel and stomping around on the mound.

When the next spring arrived, Tara began smelling a sour odor on her walk to and from the pasture each day. That was not terribly unusual, as in the country there are always wild animals wandering onto the property, and occasionally one will turn up dead in the undergrowth surrounding the pasture. She did a perfunctory search, found nothing, and decided to ignore it until one day, as she stood at the sink washing dishes, she glanced out towards the pasture, noticing something odd. She observed what looked like a dead animal lying in the middle of the walkway. She yelled at Pete to go investigate the anomaly.

But, as soon as Pete walked out the back door, Tara's curiosity overcame her, so she dried her hands and walked out onto the back porch. She could see Sundance out in the yard chewing on something, which appeared to be a dead animal. It's commonplace for Noah and Sundance to carry carcasses of dead animals that they discovered during their daily travels into the woods surrounding their property. On occasion, they have carried in antlers and even the skulls of dead animals. Pete needed to get a closer look, so he walked up and saw that Sundance was chewing on . . . Tommy's disinterred, dead body. He looked over at the place where Tommy had been buried, and all that remained of Tommy's grave was an empty hole, a big-dead-dog-sized hole. Apparently, since the spring thaw, the dogs began to smell Tommy's body, just as Tara had, so they dug until they found him and pulled him out from under the ground.

Tara couldn't resist the pull of this macabre scene, so she walked out to where Sundance was hunched over his carcass. She said, to her surprise, that Tommy looked like he did the day they buried him; his body hadn't deteriorated much, at least not visibly. Of course, he obviously wasn't buried deep enough to prevent his body from freezing over the course of the winter, which preserved his body, pretty much intact. Pete, worried that Tara might get upset, ran towards Sundance and tried to shoo him off. "Sundance!" he hissed. "Sundance, listen to me! *Quit chewing on Tommy!*" As Pete moved in to pry Sundance away from what he must've thought was quite a prize, Sundance jumped to his feet with Tommy's leg still in his mouth and started walking backwards, dragging poor Tommy's body with him. In the Labrador's defense, I'm (pretty) sure that Tommy no longer smelled like he used to and so Sundance didn't recognize him as his old friend. Sundance quickly back-stepped as Pete ran towards him, increasingly horrified at the sight. Abruptly, Tommy's leg separated from the rest of his body. Sundance took off running with Tommy's hindquarter still in his mouth. He apparently thought it was a most excellent game of keep-away, but Pete was not amused.

Needless to say, Pete climbed onto the tractor that day and dug a very deep hole to put Tommy in. He eventually recovered the separated leg from Sundance and threw that in the hole as well. And that's the story of Tommy, the Springer Spaniel. It gives a whole new meaning to the term *break a leg*. As far as Tara and Pete know, Tommy remains buried in that same spot today, but only Sundance knows for sure and he's not talking.

Some Things *are* Black and White

While the boys grew up, for five years we lived in Southern California in a three bedroom rental house with two bathrooms. Robert and I had a bathroom off the master bedroom, and the boys shared the bathroom that veered off the main hallway. The shower curtain in the boy's bathroom direly needed replacing, so I went to the store in search of a substitute. Shower curtains are feminine by nature, many of them patterned with pastel colors and flowery designs. I felt determined to find a shower curtain that was at least marginally fitting for the masculine taste. It turned out not to be such an easy task, and in fact, started what has now proved to be a lifelong challenge to hold at bay, some things that are black and white.

After visiting numerous stores, scouring shelves and racks in the linen departments, I ended up at Sears. As I approached the house wares section, I saw shower curtains hanging along the back wall. I made my way over to them and my eyes moved immediately to a black and white adorned drape. It stood out from all the others, nestled amongst its flowery pastel neighbors. The clear plastic drape had black and white penguins covering it, positioned about mid-body. The penguins had a small touch of orange on their beaks, but other than that, no additional colors. I felt the accessory would fit perfectly in the boy's bathroom, so I grabbed it, along with a trash can, a soap dish, and a toothbrush holder, all displaying the penguin theme. When I returned home, I hung the drape on the rod over the tub, as well as positioned the other accessories in their proper place. I smiled, feeling proud that I had accomplished the most important task that I had on my list that morning.

Back in the mid 1980's, penguins were not readily available as they are today. Now penguins pop up everywhere and on everything, including clothing, pictures, pillows and throws, not to mention thousands of stand-alone decorative figurines, thanks to movies like *March of the Penguins* and *Happy Feet*. But back then, every time I went shopping and spotted a black and white friend sitting on a shelf somewhere, I purchased it to add to the ambience of the boy's bathroom. I probably collected about ten or so birds, some of which sat on their vanity, while the more fragile ones I placed on a higher shelf, out of reach. The boys didn't show a lot of interest in them, not because they disliked them, but instead, the penguin theme remained background noise to the more pressing items that stole their attention, such as transformers and Legos.

When we moved to Oklahoma in 1990 and purchased a two-story house shortly after, the house had a small half-bath downstairs. The boys had grown tired of the penguin theme and since they were considerably older, voiced their desire to change the décor into something more current. I hadn't had my fill of the penguins yet, so I decided to decorate the downstairs bathroom with the black and white birds. Robert and I purchased a wall paper border that had a light blue background and filled with penguins in the foreground. I felt it added to pulling the theme together, since now the penguins permanently graced the walls of the small room. It turned out to be a convenient hobby, collecting cute animal replicas, since all my friends and relatives had something that they knew they could get me for special occasions. Well, my family and friends went a little overboard, and now the bathroom is bursting with penguins of all shapes and sizes, and in all mediums.

What started as an innocent quest to find a less-feminine shower curtain has turned into a minor obsession with cold-blooded birds that can't fly. My bathroom vanity is filled with penguin pitchers, soap dispensers and even a pen-holder from Acapulco. I have towels with embroidered penguins on them for every time of year and every holiday theme. I have a penguin rug in front of the sink and a penguin toilet seat cover, not to mention stuffed penguins lining the back of the tank. A few years back, my father decided instead of getting me more penguins for special occasions, he would build me shelves, since there was no vacant platform in which to place any more penguins. The shelves now line the walls about a foot from the ceiling, as well as along all the walls that had available space. Last Christmas when my youngest son came to visit, he disappeared for about 30 minutes into the penguin room. Concerned he might be ill, I knocked on the door to inquire about his well-being, only to be shushed by him. A few minutes later he emerged, explaining that he had been counting all the penguins in the bathroom. Including all the penguins in the pictures, (which came about when I dissected a penguin calendar, saving my favorite shots), as well as the wall-paper border, I had 711 penguins in all. I was flabbergasted to say the least, but as I thought about it, I have penguin pill boxes, nested penguins, and even a couple of snow globes. I also have penguin jigsaw puzzles that I have worked and then glued together, hanging along the lower portion of the wall. Hanging beside them are penguin pillows that we attached with string and tacked to the wall.

Did I mention the bungee penguins hanging from the ceiling? Never mind. I am sure you get the picture by now. The real question at this point is how do you get people to stop buying you penguins? I have nowhere else to put any more penguins, and to tell you the truth, my fascination with the black and white birds died, or should I say has been assassinated by an overindulgence of a good thing. What started as a mere task and slowly grew into a harmless hobby; has emerged into a full-blown obsession that's out of control. But I think the thing I fear the most is how history tends to repeat itself. You be the judge.

For Christmas a couple of years ago, I ordered a sweatshirt for my mother that had a wildlife print on it. I can't even remember what company I ordered it from, but it was one of the wildlife-themed companies like Serengeti or National Wildlife Federation. In early December, I received two boxes in the mail. One of them was a medium-sized box and the other was a long, narrow box about four feet long. It caught my attention and my curiosity grew as I started to open the box, unable to imagine what the box contained. Although, since the majority of my holiday shopping is conducted via the Internet, it's really not that unusual for me not to remember everything that I ordered. I proceeded to open the box, anticipating what treasure I would find. After successfully navigating all the plastic binding and packing tape and opening the flaps of the cardboard box, I discovered a rattan giraffe that stood about three feet tall. My first thought was that it had been delivered to the wrong house, but after verifying the address, realized that I was, in fact, the intended recipient. I then proceeded to open the second, less-curious-looking box and discovered the sweatshirt that I had ordered for Mom, along with another smaller box inside. Upon opening that box, I discovered a wooden camel with a leather saddle and harness that stood around eight inches high. I thought the giraffe looked kind of cute, but the camel seemed quite the oddity to me. I couldn't imagine who would want a camel, but then, I suppose there are a lot of people who wonder who would want a room full of penguins.

The invoice on the box had a customer service phone number on it so I called it. I explained to the gentleman that answered about the shipment and how I had received some items that I didn't order. He checked my account and corrected the bill to include only the sweatshirt. He wished me a Merry Christmas and asked if there was anything else he could do for me. I asked him what he wanted me to do with the camel and giraffe, since I didn't want them, nor did I want to pay to have them shipped back to them. He said it didn't make economic sense to ship them back, so he told me to keep the extra items. That's how my new obsession got started, with a rattan giraffe that was shipped to me by mistake.

I had bought a picture of a mother giraffe kissing the top of a baby giraffe's head a few months before, trying to fill the void on my entry-way walls. I have to say I have been fascinated with giraffes for most of my life. Their gentle and quiet nature leads me to believe that they would make the perfect pet, however impractical it may seem. But anyway, there is a small alcove in my entry-way that the stairs wrap around, so I sat the three-foot giraffe there, under the picture. It looked at home in that spot and with the picture, blending in well with its surroundings. That following spring, one of my colleagues at work brought in a fund-raising catalog for her child's school and there was a metal, wall-hanging sculpture of three giraffes included. I promptly ordered it and after receiving it, hung it on the opposite wall in the entry-way, filling in the giraffe theme. I loved the look of the alcove with the minimal giraffe trimmings, neat and uncluttered. That was five years ago. Today the alcove is bursting with shelves littered with giraffes, a cabinet with giraffes painted on it, also filled with giraffes, and a metal and glass shelving unit covered with giraffes. In addition to all the free-standing giraffes loading the shelves, I also have a six foot stuffed giraffe, a giraffe ottoman, and a smaller stuffed giraffe that swings its head back and forth while singing "Animal Crackers in My Soup". I truly started the giraffe theme in the entry-way, knowing there was limited space in the alcove, so in other words, there's not enough space available to get carried away. Perhaps, though, that line of reasoning doesn't quite make sense because my penguin bathroom is less than twenty square feet.

After Christmas last year I've had several additions to my giraffe family. I now have a giraffe tapestry, the Safari Collection from Party Lite which is giraffe-themed, a diamond giraffe pin, several giraffe Christmas ornaments, and a giraffe coat rack. It seems that history has repeated itself. The weird part is when I open a gift that contains another giraffe for my collection, I instantly adore it, even though I am out of storage space. When I smile at the giver and say, "I love it", I really mean it, even though I'm cussing them later when I'm trying to position the new animal within the herd. Oh, and speaking of last Christmas, I can't forget to add that I received another six penguins.

Recently the Tulsa Zoo had a fund-raising promotion for the new black-footed penguin exhibit. Local artists decorated penguins and these "designer" penguins were placed around town to increase interest in the zoo project. The penguins stand around eight-feet tall and I am sure weigh hundreds of pounds. The city has been auctioning off the penguins on the Internet, with bids starting at $500. I have my eye on one that is pink and carrying a purse. I am trying very hard to resist the temptation of placing a bid on her, fully recognizing, it's clearly not black and white. I guess it's time to call the doctor and get the dosage on my medication increased.

Open Wide

My experience tells me that cats really don't have belief in the Golden Rule; treat others as you would like to be treated, or in other words, don't do things to people that you wouldn't want them to do to you. My cats are very loving, although unlike dogs, very unforgiving. Unfortunately you can do just about anything to dogs and they will still love you, unconditionally, even if you act cruelly towards them. It hurts me deeply when I hear stories of cruelty towards dogs, because most of them are an easy target for bullies. On the contrary, cats never forget about, or happily adapt to, situations they do not feel comfortable with. I have to say I respect cats attitudes of not readily accepting events that do not fit within their expected norm, but at the same time, as care-givers we are sometimes forced to put cats in uncomfortable situations for their own benefit. For example, have you ever tried to give a sick cat a pill?

At the time, Mattie was a fun-loving kitten, merely six months old, when she became ill. I took her to the vet, who after a thorough examination, prescribed pills for her bacterial infection. He demonstrated with ease how to place the pill at the end of a dispenser, firmly clutching the back of her head and placing his fingers into both sides of her mouth, causing her to open wide. As she fought slightly against the pressure of his grasp, he gently placed the pill into the back of her throat and began massaging her neck until she swallowed the pill. The process seemed simple enough and as he handed me the bottle of medicine, along with the applicator, I felt convinced that I could administer the needed drug without assistance. After all, she only needed one pill a day for two weeks.

The next day when I returned home from work, Mattie greeted me as always, loudly voicing her excitement that I had returned home.

Normally the first chore of the evening was feeding the cats, but I thought I should give her the medication first and then feed her. I grabbed the dispenser and the bottle of pills, and after taking one out of the bottle, placed it on the end of the applicator. Mattie continually rubbed on my legs, pacing back and forth, in anticipation of her evening feeding. I reached down and picked her up, telling her what a good kitty she was. I noticed how little she weighed at only six months and felt relieved that she was so small and easy to handle. I felt slightly nervous about giving her the pill because I knew she would resist as she did in the vet's office. I placed her on the counter top in the kitchen, wanting her to be in a position in which I could easily constrain her. She purred loudly, pressing her head into my abdomen, which relayed her body language for "pet me". I turned her around, continually repeating loving and reassuring words to her, while securing her back half against my left side. I pressed my arm against her, so that when she struggled, she wouldn't be able to escape until I released her. I reached down with my left hand behind her head, slowly working my thumb and index finger into the opposite sides of her mouth, attempting to get her to open wide. I had the dispenser topped with the pill in my right hand so that once she opened her mouth I could quickly place the medication into the back of her throat. She struggled against being constrained, but acquiesced to the force of my fingers and opened her mouth. As I gently moved the applicator towards her, reassuring her of what a good girl she was, she chomped down hard on my thumb. As I screamed, dropping the dispenser and pulling my hand away, she securely dug her hind claws into my abdomen, launching herself off the counter and fleeing to the living room.

I looked down and could see red spots forming on my shirt, realizing that I had been injured. I walked over to the sink, turning on the faucet to wash my bleeding thumb. Grabbing several sheets of paper towel, I wrapped one around my thumb and after wetting another, lifted my shirt to wipe off the blood. I couldn't help but notice that the puncture wounds closely resembled the shape of the Big Dipper, although a scratch originating from each wound and stretched out in the direction of Mattie's departure made each one look like shooting stars. I bandaged myself up, using a couple of Band-Aids for my thumb, Since my shirt was already ruined, I left those punctures for me to deal with at a later time.

Although not wanting to, I told myself I had to complete the task at hand. I knew Mattie was sick and needed the medication, even though she violently resisted. I bent down to pick up the applicator, noticing that the pill no longer sat on the end. I looked around, searching for the pill, but couldn't find it. I picked up the rug, moved the chairs, and even got out the flashlight and peered under the refrigerator. No luck. After looking for fifteen minutes, I decided to get another pill out of the bottle. After all, there was no chance of her actually eating the pill on her own, so I didn't have to worry about her getting over-medicated.

Before I went in search of Mattie, I decided it might be wise to grab a towel from the closet for some protection against her sharp claws. I walked into the living room, calling, "Mattie, my love, where are you?" No movement. I looked behind the television, behind and under the love seat, and finally, behind the couch. I could see her crouched behind the very middle of my six-foot sofa, well out of my reach without moving the furniture. I sat down on the floor, placing the dispenser beside me, while speaking softly to her, attempting to coax her out of the safe place she had found. "Come here my sweet kitty, come to mama," I said. Mattie softly meowed and took a few steps towards me, then stopped. I continued to call to her until finally she walked towards me and crawled into my lap, purring. I petted her and scratched her under her chin, which was her favorite pastime. She rubbed against me, showing her appreciation, and I sat there on the floor stroking her, contemplating my next move. I pulled the towel around my stomach and slowly eased her between the towel and my left arm, continuing to pet her. "Yes, you're a good kitty, Mattie," I said as she looked up at me, slowly opening and closing her eyes, showing her contentment.

I almost had my fingers in her mouth when she decided it was time to make her exit, but this time I had the towel around me, so when she dug in her claws, they didn't penetrate the protective barrier I had put in place. She arched her back and tried to walk backwards, but I kept a firm grip on her, with her lodged between my mid-section and arm. I wedged my thumb and middle finger in between the opposite sides of her mouth and quickly grabbed the dispenser. Everything was going well except in my haste, I didn't have my hand completely at the end of the applicator, but instead, about halfway up. When I proceeded to deliver the medication, my index finger and thumb ended up inside her mouth, which she promptly bit down on. Immediate shooting pain ran through my hand and I released her. Of course, she promptly ran upstairs. I grabbed the towel, pressing on my flesh wounds, sorry that I had grabbed a freshly laundered white towel. I went back to the kitchen and as I stood by the sink, rinsing my gashes, a vision of the vet came to me. I quietly contemplated his every effortless move, trying to determine what I had done wrong. The most prominent thing I remembered was that he moved to place the pill in her mouth before she even opened her mouth, so I figured I took too much time trying to administer the medication. I took my time bandaging my newest wounds, giving myself time to calm down. I knew that Mattie would sense my tension if I went to her nervously. I thought, "In with the good air, out with the bad," breathing slowly and eventually regaining my composure. I felt prepared for battle, since the bandages on both hands would offer some protection against her finely-honed teeth, and with the now red and white towel as well, I had confidence I could succeed. I knew if I could find the proper motion, even once, of effectively delivering the pill, the second time would be easier. It's not like I had a choice anyway, because the only way she could recover from her illness was if I got her to take the drugs that the vet prescribed.

As I climbed the stairs with the stained towel in one hand and the applicator in the other, I walked to the bedroom at the end of the hall. I knew her favorite place of solitude was under the bed in the far corner. When I got there, I bent down to confirm that she hid under the bed. I saw her back in the corner, looking tense, and with the bed sitting against the wall, she was out of my reach. I said, "I'm sorry my sweet Mattie, but you need to take this medicine so you can get better." I wasn't sure if I could coax her out of her hiding place, knowing that I had betrayed her trust twice. I wrapped the towel around me, preparing for combat, but before I could get positioned, she charged me, wrapping both of her front paws around my right ankle, clamping down hard with those razor blades she calls teeth. I yelled, "Shit Mattie!" Instinctively, I kicked my leg, trying to remove her fangs from my flesh, extending my foot squarely into the leg of the bed. I gritted my teeth in pain, and as she released her death grip on me, I grabbed her tail, knowing if she escaped, there would be no other chance of catching her. She glared at me with her ears flattened and the hair on her back standing straight up. Then, a low, guttural growl came out of her, and unless I was there, I wouldn't have believed it possible for her to make such an unholy sound. The hair on my arms and the back of my neck stood at attention. I grasped the back of her neck, rammed my fingers into the sides of her mouth, and yelled, "Take the pill you bitch!" I shoved the dispenser with the pill on the end, back deep into her throat, not the least bit concerned about hurting her. She lashed out at me with her monster claws, tearing a new gash in my right arm. I thought, "Screw the massaging of the neck, I'm not touching that foul demon!" Confident that I had administered the medication, I released her, breathing hard but feeling relieved. She took two quick steps as if planning to flee and then stopped, coughed, and promptly spit up the pill.

She turned and glared at me, a look of hatred that I had never seen before. Instinctively grabbing her with my left hand, I lifted her by the scruff of her neck and pulled her towards me, while trying to recover the slimy pill. Not losing eye contact with her, I leaned slightly to the right, trying to grab the pill with my right hand. Before my hand reached the pill, Mattie released her bladder and voided herself freely, most of which landed on my pants. I immediately let go of her, and totally expecting a full-on blitz of her hellish fury, I raised the towel up in front of me as a make-shift barrier, but she scurried out of the room without one sound. I sat there, knowing that I had failed in my duties as a care-giver, shaking my head not sure what to do at that point. I looked over at the slimy pill lying in the middle of the bedroom and decided just to leave it for now. It became clear to me the only way she was going to get her medication was for her to eat it willingly on her own. Rising to my feet, the pain in my right toes overcame me. I shifted my weight to my heel and looked down to see the toes on my right foot swelling, knowing at that point I had probably broken at least one, if not two toes.

I contemplated searching out Mattie, not to give her a pill this time but to attempt to make amends with her. Looking down at my bleeding forearm, I decided we both probably needed a little distance, giving us time to calm down. I knew I needed medical attention, and since it was well past my doctor's office hours, I decided the closest Emergency Room was my best option. I returned to the kitchen sink, washed my newest war wound, and put some salve on it in an attempt to curtail the bleeding.

My right foot was swollen past the point of being able to put a shoe on it, but I thought I should at least put one on my left foot. I hobbled over to the desk area, where I normally leave my tennis shoes, and used my left foot to position my shoe parallel to my foot. I didn't want to bend down to assist the task with my hand, in fear of forcing pressure on my right toes that screamed in pain, so I stabilized my balance, placing my right hand on the desk area. I lifted my left foot in an effort to get it into the shoe, but without the assistance of my hand, the task proved more difficult than I expected. I wiggled the heel of my foot from left to right, slowly inching it into the shoe. When I got within an inch of my foot being fully inserted into the shoe, I pushed hard, folding the back of the top of the shoe inward. I could still feel my foot sliding slightly into place and with one last push, rammed my foot into the shoe. Instantly shooting pain ran up from the center of my heel. My immediate reaction was to remove the pressure from the left foot, so I lifted it without thinking, putting the full weight of my body onto my right foot, and onto my ever-swelling toes. Shrieks of anguished flew out of my mouth, as I fell to the ground, landing hard on my left hip upon the ceramic-tiled floor.

As tears ran down my cheeks, I grabbed the shoe and removed it with my hand, only to see the lost pill spill out onto the floor and bounce a couple of times, landing squarely in front of me, as if taunting me. Outrage rushed over me, wanting to track down the satanic witch, with visions of not shoving it down her throat but ramming it up her . . . never mind. "In with the good air, out with the bad," I thought, breathing hard. The process of putting on my left shoe while I sat on the floor proved to be much easier. I put it on, pulled myself up from the floor, grabbed my purse and keys and headed towards the garage.

Luckily, the hospital is only ten minutes from my house, so I drove up to it, parking close to the Emergency Room entrance. As I limped into the hospital, tiptoeing on my left foot to avoid my heel and walking on the heel of my right to avoid my broken toes, a female nurse ran up to me, grabbed my waist to assist me and began inquiring whether or not I had been in a car accident. I faintly smiled, not believing I could still see the humor of the situation, and stated, "No, I tried to give my cat a pill." She looked at me horrified and asked, "Lord sister, what kind of a cat do you have, a tiger?" I replied, "No, just a soldier of the devil". She spouted, "Girlfriend, how much does this cat weigh?" I looked at her sheepishly and replied, "Oh, about four pounds." She looked at me in a very pathetic, *oh you poor thing* kind of way, but then she started to giggle and so did I, just imagining what I must look like.

She walked me past the sign-in desk and straight into the Emergency Room. After getting me situated on the gurney, she started looking at the gash on my arm. I told her that wound wasn't what brought me into the ER, but instead it was the toes on my right foot. As she squatted down by my legs to look at my toes, she backed away and said, "Whew, what's that disgusting smell?" The look on her face said it all, and I started giggling so hard, I couldn't even verbalize the reason to her, not that she would really want to know anyway. She peered up at me concerned and asked, "Sweetie, did you hit your head?" I lost it at that point, howling laughter that covered the ER. She shook her head, smiled, and proceeded to bandage my wounds and fit me into a boot which would allow me to put weight on my right foot. As I regained what little self-respect I had, I left the hospital, bruised and battered. I'm sure, however, that I'm fairly lucky they didn't admit me into the psychiatric ward.

As I drove home, I decided I would not attempt to administer drugs to Mattie, or for that matter any of my cats, ever. I also decided that I would not seek her out when I got home, but instead leave her to get a good night's rest and take her to the vet in the morning to have him give her the pill. I slept restlessly that night, dealing with the throbbing toes, bruised heel and hip, and burning scratches that covered my hands and arm.

The next morning, Mattie greeted me cautiously at my bedroom door as I exited the room. I reached down slowly and petted her, re-bonding briefly with her, then carefully descending the staircase to prepare her morning meal. When she finished, I picked her up and placed her into the cat carrier that still sat in the living room from her recent trip to the vet. She meowed at me in protest, not liking the confinement, but didn't resist as I latched the door, threw the bottle of pills into my purse, picked her up and carried her to the car.

When I shambled into the vet's office, the receptionist looked at me, alarmed at my appearance. She asked, "What happened to you?" I told her it was nothing and I needed to talk to the vet. She led me into an examination room, and within a few minutes, the vet walked in. I asked him what it would cost for them to board Mattie for two weeks and administer the pills to her. He stated that the fee would be $30 per day, but attempted to relay his opinion of how unnecessary that was since I could give her the pills just as easy and not spend the money. I was relieved at that point that I didn't need crutches, because I'm quite certain I would have beaten the poor bastard to death at that point. I kept my cool though, not revealing the extent of my feline-inflicted injuries to him. I said that I had to go out of town anyway (a little white lie), so that would be very convenient to me if we could make that arrangement. He agreed. Then I inquired as to the possibility of them removing her claws while she roomed there for the two weeks. He asked, "Front or rear claws?" I said, "Every single one of them." He wrinkled his brow, probably knowing there was more to that story, but just replied that would be convenient for them. I smiled and looked at Mattie, winked at her thinking, "Serves you right," turned to him and said, "Do it".

Two weeks later I returned, still in the boot but feeling much better. After paying the $850 bill to get my cat out of jail, I took her home. She was thrilled to see me, as if nothing had happened, showing her affection by rubbing back and forth on my legs and meowing loudly. She had recovered fully from her bacterial infection, although not totally from the trauma of that torturous night. Today she's still the loving feline that I offered shelter to, at least most of the time. But every once in a while, without provocation, she'll stalk me, silently and unnoticed, jumping out from a blind spot, wrapping both her paws around one of my ankles and sinking her teeth into my flesh, while growling viscously. I've checked the calendar to see if it's a full moon in order to find a reason for her sudden outbursts of rage, but it appears her actions don't coincide with the lunar activity. I know I deserve being the brunt of her anger, after what I put her through, but I would still like to understand what prompts her at times to reflect on that incident and transform her mood from loving companion to the spawn of Satan. I clearly expect that eventually her head will spin completely around and she will start spewing pea soup out of her mouth. Maybe it's time to call in a priest.

Off Balance

I'm sure you've gathered by now that my sister is just downright crazy sometimes. That's fine with me because, throughout our lives, her antics have taken some of the focus, and sometimes some of the heat, off of me. Thus, at times, I appreciate her taking center stage. But sometimes when she tells me the stuff that happens to her, I can't help but shake my head in disbelief and wonder if either she or I was adopted. Of course, it could be that I am as crazy as a loon, just like she is, and simply don't know it. Anyway, I'll tell another story about Tara and her horses, and you can decide for yourself.

Tara doesn't function well in the morning, and I think the nicest way to put it is that she is not what people call a "morning person." Nevertheless, every morning she carries out the ritual of feeding her beloved horses as soon as her feet hit the floor. She heads downstairs and out the back door, most of the time half asleep. She has a careless habit of going out wearing only her nightshirt and a pair of panties, which usually isn't much of a problem since she lives in the middle of nowhere. She does have neighbors within visual range, but Tara's apparel isn't shocking to them any longer, as they have seen her in her undies many times. Now they just ignore her. I might also add that Tara's nightshirts are not the long nightshirts that hang down to your knees. Tara's nightshirts consist of nothing more than old T-shirts that have faded or become holey. She owns a few that actually cover her panties when she stands upright; however, the majority of them hit her about mid-hip. Since Tara isn't a particularly small person, either, you can imagine the shot that people get when she bends over with just a shirt and panties on.

This one particular morning she slipped a pair of plastic garden clogs on her feet to commence the morning rite of feeding the horses.

She made her way back to the pasture and as she scooped grain out of the feed bins, suddenly her two dogs raised their heads and looked towards the driveway. Tara's driveway is three-tenths of a mile long and covered with gravel; no one would be able to sneak up on her, at least not in a vehicle. The reactions of the two canines made Tara remember that it was time for the hay man to come and bring her monthly delivery of hay. He doesn't follow a set schedule and delivers at various times of the day. His timetable is based on his convenience, which doesn't concern Tara as long as she has hay when she needs it. So Tara never knows exactly when he will show up.

Tara froze in place, straining hear the subtle sound of an approaching vehicle. Faintly, she heard the clear sound of tires rolling over gravel. And it sounded like the vehicle traveled pretty darn fast. Tara turned to run, and when she did, her clogs slipped out from under her, just as if she was standing on a banana peel. One clog flew in front of her and the other one flew off to the side, as she tumbled upon the bony part of her knee. Tara is no spring chicken, but let me tell you, when a crisis hits, that woman can move. Abandoning the clogs, she sprang onto her feet and sprinted across her back lawn, running towards the house as if her life depended upon it. When she reached the back door, she threw it open and fell into the house, letting the door slowly shut behind her. As she tried to gather herself, she turned her head just in time to observe the hay man pulling through her backyard to deliver her hay. He carefully drove around both of her plastic clogs, which lay scattered next to the pasture fence. Tara didn't really care about them, though, because she swore that once her bruised knee healed, she would never wear plastic clogs out to feed the horses again. They were too dangerous, given her age and agility. Not only that, but she decided a trip to the local store to pick up some proper outdoor clothing topped her list of essential errands.

Tara must have thought that her current predicament did not encapsulate her ideal way to get started in the morning, especially considering she didn't really like waking up in the morning. She threw herself into a chair, still panting from her Olympic time trial and remembered that it was the 4th of July, which happened to be the day that she promised to deliver two of her horses to a perspective buyer. A few months prior a lady had given Tara a deposit and asked Tara to hold the horses while she finished building her fence. So Tara had kept the horses in anticipation of the completed barricade. With the project complete, the women decided the 4th of July holiday would be a perfect delivery date, as it fell on a Friday that year so both women had time off work due to the holiday. The three-day weekend would also allow the new owner an extra day to become acquainted with her new equines.

The perspective buyer lived in Harrisburg, about two hours from Tara's home, each way. Tara asked Pete if he wanted to ride with her, but he felt uninterested in her horse business. So Tara decided to call Anna. Tara suspects that Anna may be a distant relative, because every time Tara and Anna get together, something out of the ordinary occurs. It is almost as if some balance in the universe spins out of control. Tara doesn't appear to do anything to confront that universal shift, though, because the last time she and Anna took a road trip together, a tire on Tara's horse trailer had a slow leak. The two women repeatedly pulled into service stations along the way to keep it aired up. When they stopped at the third station, Tara's truck became lodged in the "park" position and the women couldn't move the gearshift. Second hand of course, I heard a big, burly guy stopped to help them, and after about 30 minutes of wrestling with the shifter, it finally broke lose. I guess my point is that, eventually, one of them might suggest that maybe it would be smart if they never rode together in another vehicle. I guess it's just their adventurous natures (or lunatic tendencies) that won't let them admit defeat.

Regardless of past experience, Anna said she would be more than happy to make the trip with Tara (go figure). Tara and Anna talked on the phone for almost thirty minutes plotting which route to follow. Highway 33 is a two-lane state highway, but offered the closest passage to Harrisburg. To access the expressway, they would have had to drive twenty minutes out of their way. The women decided that the best course of action would be to use Highway 33.

It just so happens, during that time, Tara had been having trouble with the taillights on her horse trailer. She swore she asked Pete to check them out and fix the problem. But either she forgot to mention it or Pete neglected to fix it, because she realized that morning that she still had malfunctioning taillights on the trailer. Determined to meet her obligation of delivering the horses, she thought that choosing to take Highway 33 was the optimal route, as the traffic would be minimal which would require less need for the taillights. That's not to say that there isn't any traffic on Highway 33, just quite a bit less than on the interstate. The worst aspect of driving to Harrisburg on 33 was that, about thirty minutes outside of town, there are some mountains that you have to traverse, and, just as with any smaller highway, the slope of the grade being much steeper than on the interstate. But all things considered (the time factor; the malfunctioning taillights; the sky-rocketing price of gas), the shorter route remained the best choice in their estimation.

The girls actually looked forward to a leisurely drive and time to discuss the problems of the world. They decided that they would leave fairly early—around 9:00 a.m.—which would allow them to be back home by early afternoon. That way, they would both have sufficient time to prepare for the evening's festivities: you know, fireworks, food, and fun (i.e., booze). They both looked forward to running a simple errand where they could catch up on everything, a lovely prelude to a holiday celebration. I don't know Anna, but truthfully, my sister Tara can talk (and talk, and talk). There is no doubt in my mind that there wasn't any dead air space in the cab of the truck that day.

About an hour into the trip, they came upon a stop sign. After briefly stopping, when Tara pushed on the accelerator again, she noticed that the truck felt strange. Tara turned to Anna and said, "I think something's wrong. The truck doesn't seem like it has any power." Anna turned to Tara and pointed out brusquely, "You've got two horses back there in the trailer; it's ninety degrees outside; and the air conditioner is running full blast. You probably *don't* have any power!" Since the truck slowly gained speed, Tara thought that maybe Anna's foresight had merit. She continued driving and, within a few minutes, the truck plowed down the road at regular speed. Tara still felt a bit concerned, though, because she knew within the next fifteen minutes they would reach the base of the mountains that lay in their path. But, by the time they got there, the vehicle seemed to be performing normally.

Her optimism was short-lived, however, because as soon as they reached the foot of the mountain and started ascending the first hill, Tara knew trouble lurked. The truck quickly lost speed, and it didn't matter how hard Tara pressed on the gas pedal, the truck didn't move any faster. In a tightly controlled, but clearly distressed voice, Tara said, "Anna, we're in trouble. I have no power." Anna looked from Tara to the speedometer and back again, realizing that Tara was right. The atmosphere in the cab of the truck quickly degenerated from barely controlled to full-out panicked. Not only did the truck continue to slow down to an alarming degree, but the road didn't have a shoulder onto which they could pull off the road. Anna yelled, "Turn off the air conditioner!" Trying to remain calm, Tara said, "You turn it off. I don't want to take my hands off the wheel or my eyes off the road." Anna quickly reached over and turned off the air conditioner, but to no avail. The truck continued to decelerate.

Tara scanned the terrain to her left and spotted a driveway. She said, "Do you think I should turn into that driveway?" The driveway was narrow and its access required Tara to make a fairly sharp turn.

Both Tara and Anna could see another road a short distance beyond the driveway. However, the stretch of highway that they were currently on had a blind curve behind them and a blind curve in front of them. Anna felt concerned that Tara would have to slow down too much to make the turn into the narrow driveway; they could end up blocking both lanes of the road if the truck lost too much momentum and stalled. The road that lay ahead offered them a wider path, allowing them to make the turn without completely slowing down. Anna said, "Let's try and make it to that road up ahead. The highway is pretty busy today and we don't want to get stuck blocking both lanes." It turned out not to be an issue one way or the other because the truck stopped before they made it to the narrow driveway, let alone the road further up the highway.

They sat there, stuck in the middle of a fairly busy two-lane highway, surrounded by two blind curves, in a stalled truck pulling a trailer with malfunctioning taillights. Tara couldn't even turn on the emergency flashers to warn anyone who approached from behind. Even if she kept her foot pressed on the brake, her brake lights wouldn't illuminate. She feared that, if people came zooming around the corner and didn't realize she was stranded, they could plow right into her. Or worse yet, they might veer into the other lane, only to discover another vehicle approaching from the opposite direction. Tara grabbed Anna's arm and yelled, "CALL 911! I'm going to get out of the truck and wave my arms to see if I can get people's attention so they''ll slow down." Anna desperately pleaded, "Oh my God, Tara, *do not* get out of the truck. YOU WILL BE KILLED!" Tara couldn't decide what to do.

Anna grabbed her cell phone out of her purse and dialed 911. When the dispatcher answered and Anna began talking, she didn't even stop to take a breath. She just screamed, "Help us! Help! We are on Highway 33 heading north and we just started to climb the mountains about thirty minutes from Harrisburg when our truck stalled. We are stuck in the middle of the road with a horse trailer attached to our truck and two horses in it, not to mention that it's 90 degrees outside and we have no water, so the horses will probably die anyway even if another vehicle doesn't slam into us and kill us all anyway. Pleeeaaasssee, help us! Help us *now*!" Anna positively begged the voice on the other end of the line. Then Anna screamed, facetiously, "Oh and by the way, my girlfriend here thinks it would be a good idea to get out of the vehicle to flag down traffic!" I'm surprised that the 911 operator took her seriously, the situation appeared so absurd, but Anna must have sounded compelling because the operator told Anna that she would notify the sheriff immediately. She also said, firmly, "Do *NOT* exit the vehicle until help arrives."

By this time Tara hung out the window waving her arms frantically, trying to attract the attention of approaching vehicles. Finally, a truck pulled up behind them with three young men inside. One of the men jumped out of their truck, walked up to the window, and asked if Tara and Anna needed some assistance. Tara said, "Yes! Yes, thank you for stopping. We thought we were going to die because we're stuck between these two blind curves." The guys took charge at that point. One of them walked towards the curve in front of the truck and one of them situated himself at the curve that lay behind the truck. The third man stood by the truck and directed traffic around it. It appeared as if they had done this before, and thus the incident quickly turned from one of sheer terror to one of minor anxiety.

Fortunately the traffic-directing crew stopped for them, because the sheriff didn't arrive for over 45 minutes. By that time another gentleman had stopped and gave them several flares to put down in the road. Tara called Pete, and even though he didn't want to, he agreed to pick them up, along with the horse trailer. Tara told him on the phone that, if he wanted to get one of his buddies to follow him, Pete and his friend could return home while Tara and Anna would take Pete's truck on to deliver the horses. In the meantime, the guy who lived in the house with the narrow driveway came out to see what caused all the commotion. After seeing the predicament they were in, he asked Tara if she wanted him to call a tow truck. She told him that would be great.

When he went back into his house to call, he disappeared for almost thirty minutes. Tara started to feel a little desperate at this point; she and Anna would probably survive but she didn't know how they were going to get the horses delivered. Finally, the sheriff showed up and asked if he needed to get a tow truck to come out. Tara told him that the gentleman who lived in the house across the way had gone inside to call one. Just after that, the gentleman returned and told Tara and the sheriff that he couldn't find anyone who would take the job. After all, it was the 4th of July. So the sheriff got on his phone and started calling towing services, in an attempt to get the incident taken care of, holiday be damned.

Then the question of the afternoon turned to the problem of how to move the trailer to a spot level enough to unhook it from Tara's truck. It had two hot and thirsty horses in it, so it needed something pretty substantial to support it. Tara and the gentleman who lived across the street walked up his driveway, discussing how they could accomplish such a task. They knew that they needed a fairly level spot to pull it off, and as any of you know who have lived at the foothills of a mountain, that is no easy feat. They finally did find a spot that they thought would work and, by the time the tow truck arrived, an hour and a half later, they knew what needed to be done.

The tow truck successfully pulled Tara's truck, trailer still attached, off the road. For the first time that day, Tara felt relieved. Her knee ached due to her nasty fall that morning, but at least she felt like she would survive the day, so she just ignored it. Pete showed up about five minutes later and they all worked together and got the vehicles switched out. Tara asked Pete where his buddy was who was supposed to take him back home, and Pete tartly replied, "I ain't settin' you two women loose with my truck. Hell, you already ruined one vehicle today, and Tara, don't forget your other vehicle is in the shop with a transmission problem." Tara got tickled and started giggling rather hysterically. Pete spoke the truth: earlier in the week her car had started acting up and the mechanic said he thought she might need a new transmission. She really couldn't blame Pete for not wanting her to drive his truck.

The rest of the story unfolded without incident. Keep in mind, though, that there was another force in play after Pete got added to the mix—a force for sane and not crazy. It wasn't merely Tara and Anna any more, alone in the vehicle, so Pete's presence brought back some balance to the universe. Needless to say, they delivered the horses later than they'd expected to, so the whole plan of having plenty of time to prepare for the evening festivities flew out the window. They didn't get home until after 5:00 that evening, so instead of slow-smoked barbecue and homemade potato salad, dinner consisted of a pepperoni pizza accompanied by a free order of bread sticks. Yum! That's more to Tara's liking anyway. She isn't much for spending time in the kitchen, so for her it turned out to be a perfect day.

Running a Cathouse

When I was a young adult, I worked with a gal, Marie, who I came to adore. She was ten years older than me and a hard-working, deep-moralled woman who I respected immensely. We became fast friends and I spent numerous evenings and weekends at her house during off-work hours. Marie portrayed the ultimate cat woman, having a minimum of twelve cats living with her at any one time, all of them stray that she could not bear to let fend for themselves. She fed them dry cat food, dumping a medium-sized bag into their trough, as she called it, which consisted of an aluminum turkey roasting pan, the ones that frequent the shelves of the local grocery stores around the holidays. I marveled at her dedication to her feline friends, even though she struggled financially at times to feed all the hungry mouths in her home. I guess she marked me, as well as my past experiences, with the undying love some humans develop for furry friends in need.

As I told you previously, Mom never allowed any animals with fur and not living in a cage to cohabitate within our household. After I left home, I welcomed the frequent visit of roaming felines on my front porch, always offering them a tasty treat while secretly hoping they would choose to stay long enough for me to offer them sanctuary inside my home. Robert brought home my first feline friend, knowing I would be pleased, and told me I needed to pick out an appropriate name. As always, at the time I was deeply engrossed in reading one of my favorite authors' books, Stephen King's Gunslinger. The protagonist and hero of the book, the so-called gunslinger, was Roland, who I quickly decided to name my new kitten after. Roland (the cat) was a white and gray tabby, short-haired and full of mischief. Along with Roland, Robert brought home food, litter and litter box, a few cat toys, and a red collar with a bell dangling from it. Roland became very comfortable living in our home, enjoying the constant attention that Robert, the boys and I gave him. Roland seemed to take on the demeanor of a gunslinger, with his sleek body and somewhat bow-legged stance; it appeared that I had picked the proper name for him.

A year later when we relocated to Tulsa, Oklahoma, we temporarily rented a very small house while searching for a place to buy. Our king-sized bed barely fit within the confines of the master bedroom. The boys shared the second largest bedroom and their furniture only fit because they had bunk beds and one small dresser that they shared. The third bedroom substituted for the storage shed that we didn't have and was filled with boxes stacked to the ceiling for all of our items that we did not have room to unpack. Saying that we lived on top of one another is an understatement, as there was virtually no vacant space in the house. Within days of moving into our new home, a Manx kitten began regular visits to our front porch. Suddenly out of nowhere, I momentarily became my mother and told the boys, "Do not bring that cat into this house!" I didn't discourage them from feeding him though and he became a scheduled evening chore, as he would appear on the front porch each evening and wait patiently for one of the boys to bring out his nightly treat. I think the arrangement with our new feline friend would have worked out as planned if it wouldn't have started raining.

The first day the rain started slowly, just a sprinkle here and there. The boys looked on the front porch and there sat their new friend, wide-eyed, awaiting their arrival. The boys voiced their concerns about the kitten sitting out in the rain. I told them to get an empty cardboard box out of the garage and make a shelter for him. They eagerly placed the box, opening towards the front door, along with an old towel for a bed, on the porch for him. As the evening wore on, the rain steadily fell harder, and the little kitten remained curled up on the towel, his new shelter working effectively against the inclement weather. Every time they would walk to the front door to check on him, he would look up at them with his big green eyes. The boys continued to express their concerns about how small the kitten looked and how cold and wet the air had become, worrying that he would get sick. I walked to the front door and gazed into those longing green eyes, and said, "Go get that cat and bring it in the house!" That is how our one-cat household became the double threat.

Again, it was my duty to name the cat and again, I knew it would come from a character out of one of the many Stephen King books I had read. The kitten, obviously male, was solid black and as I said before, a Manx. Manx cats are known as skilled hunters, so I wanted to pick a strong, male character that would well represent the newest member of the family. Dick Hallorann was a character out of *The Shining*, the first Stephen King book I read and the one that hooked me as a fan for life. In the book, Dick Hallorann is instrumental in saving the life of the mother and son (I know that's not how the movie ended, but if you haven't, try the book, the ending is much better), and not wanting to name the kitten Dick (since I mostly use that name for males I don't like), I felt Hal would be the perfect name for our new roommate.

Roland was pissed to say the least. Suddenly, his world got turned upside down by an annoying kitten who frequently pounced on him when Roland walked by, when Roland attempted to sleep, or when Roland cleaned himself. Hal defined a whole new meaning to the word mischievous, and Roland usually got the brunt of Hal's actions. Frankly, I felt bad for Roland since he had been the only cat in the house for the first two years of his life, and just like an only child, was not used to sharing our attention or getting picked on. Hal would wait patiently behind a door for Roland to walk by. Hal didn't need to see him to know he was there, since the bell on Roland's collar jingled as he walked, and as Roland approached the edge of the door, Hal would jump out at him, usually launching Roland airborne. After the hissing and the spitting subsided between the two of them, they would each go their separate ways until the next surprise attack. This went on for weeks until I became annoyed and formulated a plan. I went to the pet shop and bought another collar with a bell on it. When I got home I placed it around Hal's neck, smiling as I thought, "Now you can see how it feels." I suspected that he wouldn't be able to hide from Roland without detection, since he now had an alarm around his neck. The strange thing that happened was that Roland didn't even seem to notice the sound of the bell around Hal's neck. I guess because Roland became so used to hearing his own bell, he didn't distinguish the familiar sound of the bell between his and Hal's jingles. Hal would walk down the hall, completely alone, and abruptly shoot straight up in the air, flipping and hissing, and after landing, looking frantically around as if someone stalked him. It happened most of the time when Hal would pass a doorway and his aerobatic actions became quite comical. At first, I thought, "That cat is possessed." But then it dawned on me that when he heard the bell jingle, he immediately suspected it was Roland's bell, and since when it jingled, he knew the bell was in close proximity, he panicked and reacted crazily. Needless to say, the family experienced many moments of amusing tricks caused by the jingle bells.

We allowed the cats to wander outside into the back yard. Numerous trees lined our property and as you would suspect, numerous birds lived in those trees. Hal would strut through the backyard and the fearless birds would dive down towards him, sometimes swooping just out of his reach. Others would actually nip at his butt, then climb through the air quickly as Hal flipped around in an attempt to capture his feathered attackers. Hal did prove to be the skilled hunter of his breed over time, and would frequently leave us a present on the back porch, proudly displaying the result of his quick reflexes. The first time I encountered a dead bird on the back porch, I screamed, alarmed at the sight. I scolded Hal for his uncaring act, but it didn't faze him one bit. It seemed he heard nothing and didn't feel any shame for his mindless deeds, as he continued to strut across the yard, as if enticing the birds to get close. Sometimes I wondered if Hal didn't have a bit of the "shine", just as his namesake who foresaw future events, since sometimes Hal moved in for the kill before the birds reached him, as if he knew what was going to happen in advance.

That was thirty years ago and although I've managed to keep the feline count way below twelve, I understand what drove my friend Marie to take care of so many friends in need. She couldn't say no to a cat without a home and neither can I. I also understand my mother's refusal to allow fur-bearing animals inside her home. Since I work full-time outside the household in the corporate world, I set aside the weekends for most of the household chores, such as vacuuming. I can tell you that having several cats living with me creates a challenge, as often by the end of the week the dust bunnies are bigger than the felines who created them. Although must admit I feel at peace knowing that at least I don't have to feed them. As far as the rest of the feline clan, sadly, many of them have passed over the years, but I like to believe that it's God's way of making room for the next feline in need. Or possibly since I don't have the ability to turn away a stray animal, it may be his way of ensuring my sanity by not allowing too many animals into my life.

Throughout those thirty years I have had many cats bless my home that are no longer with me. Jake (named after the young boy who was Roland's companion in the Dark Tower series) was a gray, tiger-striped cat who had a calm and level-headed demeanor. Nothing seemed to bother him. He wasn't a bit nervous like some of the other feline's I've had grace my home. Jake was a loyal friend and a constant companion, much like that of the young boy I named him after.

Oy (named after the billy-bumbler in the same Stephen King series, who was Jake's dedicated, loving, and constant companion) had solid black fur and stayed constantly energetic. He never missed an opportunity to play the *class clown* and remained underfoot whenever I was home. That is, unless I sat in my favorite chair, at which time he would curl up on my lap, always demanding my affection.

Church (named after the cat in Pet Cemetery) was a long-haired, gray tiger-striped feline. Church displayed some disturbing behavior early in life. I rescued Church from a family who kept her locked in the basement, so she was not used to being around people. She definitely had a spooky side to her, and sometimes leaned towards schizophrenic tendencies. It seems bazaar to me that the cats I have named after characters from books tend to take on some of their characteristics. Maybe it's my imagination or just my perception that they portray characteristics of the fictional beings that Stephen King brought into my life, or on the other hand, maybe it's just karma.

Today I have four cats, three of which are named after Stephen King characters. Charlie is an orange, tiger-striped tabby who I named after the Fire Starter, Charlene whose father called her Charlie. I thought Charlie was a girl when I first got him (sorry Charlie), but later found out that in fact, he was male, although the name Charlie still fits perfectly I picked the name because Charlie's fur is a vibrant, deep orange, much like the color of fire, although his personality is intense, very strong and independent. He marches to his own beat regardless of what the other felines are doing, although he's been known to disrupt their solitude in a flash. I think it's his way of demanding control of the herd, which fits the group well since all packs need a leader.

Reah is a black and white long-haired cat who I named after the witch in the Dark Tower series. My girlfriend brought Reah to me after she had found her in the middle of the road, bleeding from an animal attack. She was only about six weeks old, and I took Reah to the vet and got her stitched up. She survived with nominal damage, specifically she is missing part of her upper lip. I call her my lipless wonder, because I think it's a wonder she survived a vicious animal attack at such a young age. I named her Reah because of her black fur, but with her face disfiguration, people probably think she looks a little like a witch, but she's beautiful to me.

Mattie is a calico cat and came to me from a neighbor lady whose cat had kittens and her husband was going to take them out and shoot them if she didn't find homes for them. Mattie was a character in Stephen King's Bag of Bones. I fell in love with Mattie when I read the story and also fell in love with Mattie the cat the minute I laid eyes on her. She was one of the most loveable kittens I had ever encountered. Maybe she thought I was her mother, but she used to suck on my shirt tail while she flexed her paws, as if she were nursing. As she grew up, she has developed quite the attitude (as referenced in my previous story) and is not as fun-loving as when she was a kitten, but still loveable none the less.

I live in a rural area and have about an acre fenced, the perfect yard for a dog to thrive. I got a call from the Border Collie rescue, saying that their facilities were full and they needed to find a home for a six-month old Border Collie. I agreed to meet the dog. When the gal brought her into my home and took her out the back door into the yard, I was surprised at how well behaved she acted, as well as calm while she was being introduced to a new environment. I asked the gal what the dog's name was and she said "Mattie". I smiled, knowing that she probably already belonged to me in spirit. She definitely had the right name, although, left to me I would have picked something different than the name already belonging to one of my feline friends. She fit in quickly and I agreed to take her. It's kind of fun to stand at the back door and yell "Mattie"! Both the dog and the cat come running (I know, sick amusement, but remember, I fell on my head when I was little). I know now that the tradition of naming cats will now be bestowed upon my canine friends as well, it just seems like the natural thing to do (although there's no way I'm ever getting a St. Bernard!)

I guess I have to finish by telling you about my fourth cat, Venus. When my son Jess was still in middle school, he said he wanted a white cat for his birthday. During the next week while still taking his request under consideration, Jess came home from school and said someone had dumped a calico kitten at the school. He said that his teacher was caring for the kitten, but needed to find a permanent home for the cat. Jess said if I let him bring it home, that would satisfy his request for a white kitten, although the calico was only partially white. He insisted on naming the cat, not liking my choice of names, so he named the cat Venus (of course, not a Stephen King character). As you might guess, when he grew up and left home, he left Venus with me. She's 17 years old and going strong, other than the fact that I had to cut off her tail because she had chewed on it to the point of killing it, but that's a whole new story in itself. Regardless, she's in better health than my other three, although older. I suspect she will outlive her younger siblings. I wish Stephen King would write a book including a female character called Venus, just so I can get my universe back in sync.

Bargain Hunting

Robert always fondly asserted that I couldn't pass up a good bargain, and that my head contained a force that magnetically pulled me towards the word "sale" printed anywhere. Although I don't contest his perspective, I lovingly refer to this condition as my sale gene. It is inherent to my genetic code and I have no control over the disorder. In contrast, my sister Tara did not get blessed with the sale gene. She would much rather pay full retail for an item than search the earth for a twenty-percent off sale. I'm aghast at the thought of paying full price for anything. I don't know who gets a bigger kick out of my malady, Robert or Tara.

I have withstood my share of grief from both of them over the years about buying reduced-priced products in quantity. I prefer to call it "stocking up." Robert has, on many an occasion, alluded to it as "insane." Perhaps there *are* times that his description more accurately describes my obsession. For example, I do seem to remember a time when we had about fifty cans of Bumblebee tuna in the cupboard because it had been on sale for a couple of weeks. I couldn't resist the urge of picking up a few cans every time I stopped at the store for bread or milk, or (if I am going to be totally honest) any time that I passed within a five-mile radius of the grocery store.

Robert and I lived in Southern California in the late eighties, and during that time, the Orange County Swap Meet was the best place to satisfy my hunger for bargains. It comprised several square miles in the middle of Orange County and operated every weekend. Vendors rented space and sold their various wares under portable awnings that protected them from the elements; at the Swap Meet, you could literally see an ocean of such awnings, hundreds of them. As you can imagine, a visit to the Orange County Swap Meet consumes the entire day. You can't just drop in for a few minutes to have a quick shopping experience. The experience requires at least ten or fifteen minutes just to locate a parking space and walk in. It's all worthwhile, though, because you can find a miscellany of items, from common everyday goods like cookware and linens to one-of-a-kind vendible's, such as hand-painted articles like bird houses and even t-shirts.

Needless to say, the Orange County Swap Meet was our favorite Christmas shopping locale. It offered a good selection of crafts and other distinctive items that you couldn't purchase anywhere else, and, since hundreds of dealers vied for business, the products were competitively priced. That in itself was enough to inspire me to venture into the maze of the Swap Meet. Robert also enjoyed going, but not necessarily for the same reasons I loved it; I believe Robert enjoyed the Swap Meet so much because it contained a huge selection of electronics. The Swap Meet probably sold more audio and video equipment than any other type of merchandise, and Robert adored perusing the various stands for the latest technological discovery, nearly always finding good deals if he searched long enough.

One weekend we traveled to the Swap Meet with the goal of accomplishing some early Christmas shopping. In addition, our telephone at home desperately needed replacement. The number five button stuck, and often when you pressed it, it reacted as if it had been pressed two or three times. Other times it wouldn't respond at all, as if you had never touched it. Knowing that the Swap Meet housed many people selling telephones, our primary quest for the day consisted of acquiring a replacement phone. Any other various sundries that we stumbled upon in the meantime we'd consider an added benefit, but we needed to purchase a new phone above all else.

As with many ventures like the Swap Meet, the vendors who sell similar items do not congregate in one area. There is no rhyme or reason to the order in which the space is configured and the way the dealers position themselves. The spaces are rented on a first-come, first-serve basis, and whoever leased a particular space would simply set up shop with whatever wares he or she intended to sell. The area resembled a concrete labyrinth, and in order to shop for any specific item, you were forced to weave your way through the cement maze, like a worker ant on a glass-walled farm, if you wanted the best deal. And that was exactly what we did that day, just like on any other day we visited the Meet.

If you walk briskly and stay focused, it is possible to navigate through the Orange County Swap Meet in about four hours. This assumes that you investigate each seller and check prices on similar items. Immediately as we entered the front gate, a vendor stood in the first stall selling touch-tone telephones. I inquired about the price of this particular vendor's phones. He replied, "$12.95 for all the phones, except for the red ones. They're $14.95." I thought, "What an odd comment", since I didn't consider red to be an appealing color for a phone. After pondering his response for a few minutes, unable to arrive at a logical reason as to why the red phones were more expensive, we decided to ignore the oddity and continued our quest for the best-priced (and less emergency-looking) phone.

As we approached the next booth selling telephones, I asked the attendant what his phones cost. He replied, "$12.95 for all the phones, except the red ones. They're $14.95." Again, being puzzled, I thought his response was peculiar for a couple of reasons. First, the price of his phones was exactly the same, down to the penny, as the first vendor's prices. Second, both guys charged a $2.00 premium for the red phones. I turned to Robert and said, "Who on earth would want a red phone in their house?" He shook his head in agreement at the oddity of the coincidence and acted equally curious as to what could cause this new fixation on red phones. I stood there for a few minutes, resting my left hand on my hip, and gently rubbed my chin with my right hand in contemplation.

A discussion ensued between us as to why people choose a particular color for their phone. We agreed that the majority of people want to match the color of their phone with the décor of the room in which it resided. I envisioned mostly neutral colors, such as white or brown, or even brighter colors such as blue or yellow, which wouldn't be out of place in a kitchen or living room, but I couldn't imagine red matching much of anything in the way of home decor. Then I thought maybe the fixation developed out of a fascination with what turned me off of the color: perhaps people *were* pretending to be President, imagining that their bright red phones were symbols of importance and decision-making of the highest order. Robert and I agreed that it could be a new kind of (odd) status symbol. We both started giggling at such as idea, and as we strolled along, I broke into the theme from "Secret Agent Man." ("Hello? James Bond here. What can I do to help you, Mr. President?")

We visited every booth that day, and all the phones had the same price—except for the red ones, which cost $2.00 more. Every time the people in the booths said, "except for the red ones," Robert and I looked at each other and smiled. It became pretty entertaining actually, very droll. At some point, we really wanted to repeat "except for the red ones" along with them, but thought the sales people might think we were making fun of them. Our amusement increased as each booth attendant intoned the same words throughout the day. The most questionable part of the whole incident was that there was no shortage of red phones on display. Obviously, the vendors had plenty of red phones to sell, so it didn't appear to be a supply and demand issue. By the same token, we didn't have any trouble believing there might be a surplus of red phones, since the dealers asked a premium for them.

As we neared the end of Swap Meet, the last booth next door to the exit gate housed another electronics dealer with a slew of touch-tone phones on display. Robert and I decided earlier that, since everyone sold phones for the same price, we would buy one towards the end of the Swap Meet, so we didn't have to lug it around with us all day. We walked up to the person in the booth and I asked him how much he wanted for his phones. He replied, "$12.95." I paused for a few seconds, waiting for him to say, "except for the red ones," but he just looked at me expectantly. I asked, "Even for the red ones?" He replied, kind of puzzled, "Yeah, they're all the same price, regardless of what color they are." I said, "I'll take a red one." I paid him the $12.95, and he handed me the bag with my new red phone. I beamed with pride, as I turned to observe Robert standing there with his arms crossed and his eyebrows raised. I looked up at him and demanded, "What?", all the time knowing exactly what he thought. He said, "What in the world are you doing buying a *red* phone? Didn't we just say that the *red* phone goes with nothing in our house? Have you lost your mind?" I spluttered, "But . . . but . . . it was on sale! What did you expect me to do?" Robert just stood there, staring at the ground and shaking his head in disbelief. He knew that the powerful urge created by my sale gene clearly controlled my actions that day, and therefore, he was destined to have a red phone in his house. Reflecting on the situation, I even have a hard time believing that I bought the damned red phone that day. I didn't even want a red phone, but I guess my genetically encoded drive got the best of me. I don't know if the uncontrollable sale gene reared its ugly head (probably) or the idea that this phone could be a status symbol (less likely), but I do know is that it just seemed like the appropriate decision at the time.

I still have that red phone. It no longer works, but I just can't bear to part with it. Every time I see the phone sitting on the shelf in the closet, I think of that day and smile, remembering the series of events that led up to its purchase. When Robert and I returned home from the Swap Meet that afternoon, I couldn't wait to call Tara and tell her the whole saga of the red phone. Although I knew I would take some ribbing about it from her, I just couldn't resist bragging about my conquest. I think she's still laughing.

You Can Never Be Too Thin

Although Tara and I are similar in many ways, one thing that we have always been opposite in is our body structure. I have been blessed with a fairly slender body, along with small bones. To the contrary, Tara has been cursed with a large frame, big bones, and the body mass to go with them. As a result, Tara has been on and off one diet or another her entire life. During our teenage years, no different from today, one fad diet after another became popular. Tara attempted them all. I even remember one called the Spit Diet. The whole basis of that diet was never to swallow your saliva. Whenever you collected a mouthful of saliva, you were supposed to spit it out instead of swallowing it. It may not have made anyone terribly thin, but it kept its participants constantly busy, not to mention the fact that they made a real spectacle of themselves in public places. But Tara willingly tried all the diets at least once, and some multiple times, just to convince herself that she gave it a thorough effort.

Now that Tara is in her sixties, she continues experimenting with one diet or another. Heidi, Tara's youngest daughter, said to Tara one day, "Mom, you've been on a diet my whole life." Tara responded by saying, "Yeah, and just think how big I would be if I hadn't been dieting all those years!" Tara keeps a pretty good sense of humor about her weight, as with most everything else in her life, as you can probably already tell by some of the previous stories about her. In her younger years, she was more self-conscious about it. Today, it's just a fact of life to her. I think she may have finally reached the conclusion that being healthy and happy is more important to her than being thin. Of course, this also allows her to keep her current habits and indulge in all the delicious food that she would otherwise miss out on.

During one of her weight-loss episodes, she asked her husband Pete if he had any ideas about what she could try next. Pete told her that he had this gadget called the *Belly Buster*. He explained that, when he wore it to work, he always lost weight in his abdominal region. In fact, he said that sometimes he lost as much as two inches in one day. Remember, Pete is a pretty big guy who weighs around 300 pounds. So Tara didn't expect that she would lose two inches in one day, but after Pete's dissertation, she became immediately interested in giving the *Belly Buster* a whirl.

One morning soon after their conversation, as Tara got dressed for church, she went downstairs and asked Pete where he kept his *Belly Buster* device. She thought she would wear it to church that morning. It was wintertime, and she planned to wear a sweater and a wool skirt, so she thought that the device wouldn't be noticeable under her heavy clothing. Pete told her that he kept it in the top drawer of his dresser with his socks and underwear. Tara went back upstairs to get it.

She pulled it out of the drawer and examined it with curiosity. It consisted of a continuous piece of rubber, like a fan belt for a car, except the *Belly Buster* was about six inches wide. It didn't have a zipper or Velcro on it, but on one side of it, there was a cloth covering, which resembled cheesecloth. Earlier, Pete had informed her that in order to put it on, you step into it with the cloth side towards your body. After you pulled it over your hips, close to your waist, you flipped it over so that the smooth, rubber surface lay against your skin.

Tara attempted to pull the Belly Buster up to her hips. She had never possessed a great deal of upper body strength, so she pulled and tugged, but only managed to get it up to her knees. Determined to try the device, she continued tugging and pulling, first on one side and then on the other. After several minutes of struggling with it, she succeeded in getting it just above her knees. She realized that her effort to raise the contraption over her hips was futile without some outside help. In the meantime, she had gotten herself into quite the predicament. The rubber belt was designed to fit tightly, of course. She had managed to position the constrictor around her knees, where it fit so snugly that her feet struggled to stay far enough apart to keep her balance.

Tara yelled downstairs for Pete and told him that she needed assistance. As Pete climbed the stairs, he heckled Tara, calling her a sissy, and told her that he had lost patience her whining; *he* could manage the *Belly Buster* all by himself. Of course, Tara expected his comments, since she and Pete banter back and forth constantly. He walked into the bedroom, grabbed the *Belly Buster* and yanked it up. He completely lifted Tara off the ground and, with his hands firmly gripping the rubber belt, began jouncing her, just as if he were shaking a pillow into a pillowcase. Her hips slipped right through it and the Belly Buster ended up just barely below her waist. Then Pete took the edge of it and flipped it over so that the rubber side of the *Belly Buster* rested against Tara's skin.

And, man it felt tight—*really* tight! Tara turned to Pete and said, "How in the hell did you ever get this on?" She felt as if she could hardly breathe and couldn't imagine Pete getting the device on, not to mention wearing it all day and working in it. After all, he did weigh almost twice as much as Tara. Pete just grinned and continued to accuse Tara of being a big sissy with no fortitude. And Tara really couldn't argue with this, as she could barely breathe, so she finished dressing and they hurried off to church.

Tara said that, the entire time they sat in church, the only thing that she could think about was getting home and taking that damned thing off. It fit extraordinarily snugly. In fact, the *Belly Buster* fit so tight it hurt, but she persevered and tried listening to the sermon. That day she felt closer to Jesus than she ever had, such was her suffering. She made certain that anything she had ever done that might need explaining was thoroughly explained in her prayers; she needed to make sure she had closure, just in case. She started feeling as if she was going to be cut in two and wasn't sure that she could endure the agony the rest of the morning. By the end of the service, she worried about even surviving the trip home, so she felt good that she had (hopefully) made her peace with the big guy.

When she and Pete got home, Tara ran into the house and up the stairs. She started shedding clothes before she even reached the bedroom. After she had removed her skirt and sweater, she began tugging on the rubber belt, trying to relieve the tension. She couldn't get it to budge, not even an inch, let alone remove it altogether. Finally, she decided that she would try to roll it down her body, but that turned out to be a very bad idea. Once she had rolled it down, it resembled a bicycle inner tube, and it became even more rigid and unyielding. The more she struggled, the tighter the grip on her torso became.

She felt increasingly alarmed and started yelling for Pete. She realized that she was not capable of removing the *Belly Buster* on her own, which she should have known since she couldn't even get the thing on without some help. Pete came up the stairs, smarting off with his sissy comments, and arrived at the doorway. He walked in and had to do a double take when he saw the rubber belt rolled up like an inner tube. He began tugging on the contraption, but it wouldn't budge. He couldn't even get it unrolled. It seemed as if it had permanently affixed itself to Tara. Despairingly, she pleaded, "Get this thing off of me," as her voice quivered. Every attempt that Pete made was in vain.

Finally, after about five or ten minutes with no progress, Pete got frustrated. Tara kept asking him over and over again, "How did you ever get this thing on, let alone off?" He just glared at her without responding. He became fed up with the whole situation, and pulled out his pocketknife, pointing it towards the rubber tube. Tara screamed, "Don't cut me! Be careful!" It appeared as if her body slowly absorbed the rubber gadget, and her flesh began to overlap the belt; it was only a matter of time before her body sucked up the rubber tube entirely. Pete carefully took his knife and cut the piece of rubber in two. The belt immediately flew across the bedroom, struck the wall with a loud thwack! and landed in the corner, a heap of floppy rubber. Pete strode over to it and snatched it off the floor in a huff.

A sense of relief washed over Tara. She was finally able to catch her breath and felt the panic slowly subsiding. Pete walked over to his dresser, angrily tossed his pocketknife onto the top, and yanked the top drawer open. As he went to throw the now unusable rubber belt into his top drawer, he froze in place. He looked from the drawer to the rubber belt hanging in his hand, and then back again. Finally, as Pete stared down at the limp piece of rubber in his hand, he exclaimed, "MY THIGH THING!" Tara looked at him, puzzled, and said, "What?" Pete yelled, "MY THIGHT THING! YOU'VE RUINED MY THIGH THING!" Tara responded, "What thigh thing?" Spittle spewed from Pete's mouth as he yelled, "*THIS THIGH THING!*" Apparently, not only was Pete's *Belly Buster* still in the top drawer of his dresser, the so-called "thigh thing" usually resided there as well. The thigh thing looked identical to the *Belly Buster*, although it was designed for wearing on a person's thigh when they had an injury. Pete had pulled a groin muscle from an accident he had at work a while back, and had worn the thigh thing around his leg to help support his muscle during healing. As it turned out, all morning Tara had been wearing what she had thought was the *Belly Buster*, but it was really a rubber belt made to support a man's thigh. All Tara could do was shake her head and turn on Pete, "Yeah, and who's the sissy now, you whiner!"

I bet she must have felt pretty good that day, knowing that she hadn't imagined the pain. She had to be fairly proud of herself after enduring the discomfort of a thigh-sized belt worn around her waist for a couple of hours. Talk about fortitude! I also think that was the beginning of her realization that all her struggles to be thin progressed a bit too far. I love her just the way she is, but more importantly, I think she is starting to love herself that way, too.

A Place Setting for Four

I fanatically plan everything. The only way I can stay organized and guarantee that my tasks get completed in the time I have available is by planning. But as hard as I try to keep control, things don't always go as planned. Even worse, it seems that some days when one thing goes wrong, everything begins to go wrong; the "snowball effect" takes hold. When the snowball starts rolling downhill, it picks up more and more bad karma along the way, creating more and more chaos in the universe. The whole ordeal becomes increasingly alarming, since once the snowball starts down the slope, you never know when it will stop. It could end up as a medium-sized snowball, which I might add is still no picnic, but at least it's not the avalanche it sometimes turns into. On one day in particular, the only thought in the forefront of my mind was of having a nice, quiet evening at home with friends. It seems simple enough, doesn't it? And it most certainly would have been—had I not decided to purchase new flatware for dinner that evening.

I had become good friends with Steve, a guy that I worked with, and so I suggested that he and his wife, Janice, spend the evening with my husband, Robert, and me. He quickly checked with her and, after she concurred, we planned our get-together. Janice and I had never met, but when Steve described her personality, I thought it would fit well with mine. From what he revealed about her, I had the impression that her demeanor may be a little more reserved than mine, and I made a mental note to make sure everything was in order so she would feel comfortable in our home for the evening. Since Steve and I meshed so well, we hoped that we could all have an enjoyable evening together.

Preparing for the evening began the night before, on a Friday. After work, I busily tidied up the kitchen, unloading the dishwasher that I had run that morning. When I started putting away the silverware, I noticed that little rust-colored stains had formed on almost all the pieces, and after closer examination, I realized that the plating on the utensils had been penetrated. This irritated me because I had only purchased the utensils about a month earlier. But that wasn't the worst part of it. Six months earlier, I had bought another eight-piece place setting from the same store. It was a different design, but cost about the same. That set had deteriorated just as rapidly. I didn't return the first set to the store because, upon reading the packaging after I started having the problem, I noticed that the manufacturer discouraged the use of lemon-scented dishwashing soap. And of course, that was what I used, so I just assumed that the soap had caused the problem. After I purchased the second set of silverware, I carefully selected a different type of dishwashing liquid, making sure that I never bought anything that contained lemon as an ingredient. Switching dishwashing liquids aggravated me the most, thinking that I had caused the issue by not reading the warnings on the package, but then after correcting the so-called culprit of the problem, the second set deteriorated just as quickly.

That evening I decided that the next morning I would go to an up-scale department store and purchase a new set of silverware. I also decided that I would return *both* sets of flatware that I had purchased from the first store and get a refund. By doing that, the more expensive, and hopefully more durable, set of flatware would use less out-of-pocket cash. Truthfully, though, the real reason I wanted to return the defective utensils was to try to convince myself that I didn't make a completely idiotic decision by purchasing another cheap set of flatware from the same store after the first set only lasted a few months. I spent the rest of the evening collecting all the pieces and packaging them up, preparing to take them back to the store the day of our little dinner party.

That morning I drafted myself a list of errands. I knew that I would be running around like a crazy woman, so I decided to skip my shower until later. I knew that the store to which I needed to return the silverware opened at 8:00 in the morning, so at 7:45, I pulled out of the driveway. I kept going over the list in my head: return the silverware, drive into town, buy new flatware, go by the liquor store, purchase a couple of bottles of good wine, and end at the grocery store to buy the food for dinner. My ultimate goal was to return home by noon so that I would have plenty of time to shower, prepare dinner, and relax for a little while. Steve and Janice were scheduled to arrive around 6:00 that evening, so I felt certain that I would have plenty of time to accomplish my agenda.

I arrived at the first store at 8:00 that morning on the dot. I entered the store and went to customer service, where I explained the problem with the flatware to the clerk. I also told her that I wanted a refund for obvious reasons. She nodded in agreement, but when she scanned the barcode, the system did not recognize the UPC symbol. She then picked up a catalog and went in search of the price for the two sets of silverware so that she could comply with my request. After having no luck at finding a match, she sent another clerk to the house wares department in search of a duplicate set. The second clerk returned after an extended absence, shaking her head, indicating that no similar sets existed on the shelf. She returned carrying a set that the same manufacturer produced, but in a different design. Enough difference remained between the two sets that the clerk then called the store manager. After many lost minutes of deliberation, a call to the corporate office, and the aid of another member of management, they decided that they would just refund the current price of the flatware that the clerk had retrieved from the shelf. I fought the impulse to get aggravated, because I knew the confusion partially resulted from my actions since I had delayed returning the merchandise. However, I became thankfully relieved when the clerk handed me the cash, since I didn't want to waste another precious minute.

I hopped into my car and, in no time, I was back on the freeway. I knew that driving into the city would cost me extra time, but I also knew that it would be worthwhile. I had seen a set of flatware that really caught my eye a few months before, and I knew that the next time I needed new cutlery that style would be at the top of my wish list. The utensils were made from a heavier metal, and therefore, they should be more durable. When I got to the store, the clock inched well past 9:00 that morning. I started to visualize *the snowball slowly rolling down the hill*, but hastily pushed the thought away. I rushed into the store and proceeded to the counter. The layout of the store resembled a warehouse where you placed your order, paid for it, and then received a number. When they serviced your request, your merchandise came out of the warehouse on a conveyor belt. I walked up to the counter, ordered two *place settings for four* of the flatware, and paid for them. The clerk handed me my ticket, and I commenced to chomping at the bit while pacing back and forth. I tried to occupy myself by pretending that I had an interest in other merchandise that sat out on display, but I knew that time kept creeping inexorably by.

After what seemed like an extraordinarily extended amount of time, I realized that the three people who stood in line behind me when I ordered had already picked up their merchandise and left the store. *The snowball was picking up speed.* I marched up to the counter and asked the clerk to check on my order, so she placed a call to the warehouse. About five minutes later, two boxes of silverware emerged on the conveyor belt. Relieved that my order had arrived, I retrieved the boxes and dashed out of the store in a flash. As I drove through town towards the freeway on-ramp, I glanced down at my watch. What I estimated would take me an hour had taken me over two. I continued to reassure myself that I still had plenty of time, and could possibly even make up some time at the grocery store. I had two more stops to make and less than two hours to make them in if I was going to achieve my goal of returning to my rural home by noon.

My next stop was essential: the liquor store. I told myself before entering that I wasn't just going to grab the first two bottles of Merlot I encountered. I wanted to browse and choose two bottles that I and my guests would really relish. Luckily enough, I was in and out of the liquor store in less than fifteen minutes with a lovely bottle of Sonoma County Sebastiani and another of Napa Valley Beringer. That meant that I still had an hour and fifteen minutes to accomplish my grocery shopping and return home.

Unfortunately, I knew immediately that I trouble lurked when I had to park a half-mile from the store. This particular grocery store's parking lot encompassed an immense amount of acreage, and I had to park on the outer perimeter: clearly, everyone in the greater metropolitan area planned to host a dinner party that evening. In spite of this, I remained upbeat. I knew that I was only ten minutes from home at this point, and even if shopping took longer than I expected, I had plenty of time to get everything done once I got home. After picking up all the items on my grocery list and standing in line for approximately twenty minutes, I exited the grocery store with a sigh of relief. By this point noon had come and gone, but with my errands complete and returning home shortly after, I realized that I had only missed my goal by thirty minutes. I had five and a half hours to shower, prepare dinner, and relax. It was completely possible, not a problem at all. I congratulated myself on my planning expertise.

I unpacked the groceries and carefully arranged the various dinner items together on the counter: first, I needed to season the steaks so they had time to sit and soak up the spices; second, I would prepare the potatoes and fresh vegetables for roasting, and finally, I would prep the ingredients for the Caesar salad. I didn't want to start cooking until I took a shower, but I wanted to be organized once I started. Above all, I wanted to unpack and wash the new utensils before taking a hot, relaxing shower and maybe a quick nap. I opened the box and gently slid the silverware out. Each piece had an individual plastic sleeve around it. I removed each sleeve and put each utensil in the sink, preparing to wash them. When I finished emptying the first box, I proceeded to the next box. About halfway through the second box, an uneasy feeling started to grow in the pit of my stomach; something wasn't adding up. Finally, it struck me: I couldn't remember handling many butter knives. I walked over to the sink, and although I saw four dinner forks, four salad forks, four tablespoons, and four teaspoons, there were only two knives.

I started to feel tense—you know, that feeling you get just before full panic mode sets in. Your heartbeat races and you become a little short of breath. I still had half of the second box to get through, so maybe it wasn't quite time to panic yet, but my palms had broken out in a sweat. I ripped the rest of the silverware out of the box and started frantically tearing the plastic sleeves off of each utensil. I searched desperately for knives, more knives, but when all of the silverware was unpacked, I had only five butter knives. It wouldn't have been such a big deal—two dinner guests, Robert, and me—except for one small problem: did I forget to mention that my parents had a habit of dropping by on the weekends? In fact, we could almost count on it. That adds up to six people for dinner and only five knives. *The snowball began to charge down a very steep hill.* The two sets supposedly had eight of each utensil, four in each package. But instead, there were only two knives in the first box and three knives in the second box. Fear paralyzed me. I had just returned all the silverware I owned and replaced it with two incomplete sets. My dinner guests were due to arrive in less than six hours and I didn't have enough flatware.

I quickly began sorting silverware and made the decision to return to the city and replace the deficient set. I knew that at a minimum I needed six of each utensil, and so I figured I would segregate four of each utensil and return whatever number was leftover back to the store, in effect keeping one full set and returning one deficient set. I managed to effectively separate four of each type and left them in the sink. Then I grabbed a plastic grocery bag and, not bothering to repack the goods, I threw in the rest of the utensils, along with a handful plastic sleeves and one of the opened boxes. I flew out the back door, jumped into the car, and took off for the city, which was—inconveniently and for the second time that day—more than thirty minutes from my rural home.

By the time I arrived at the store, the clock had struck 1:30 p.m. Sullen about the whole incident, I walked into the store and marched directly to the counter where I had purchased the substandard sets. I don't think it takes a rocket scientist to figure out that both sets of utensils I had purchased had already been returned by another customer, thus explaining the missing knives. I did, however, get a vision in my head of some nitwit sitting in the back room sorting a big, jumbled pile of flatware into boxes after they received my order earlier that day. Maybe that would explain the extraordinary amount of time it took for the order to materialize from the conveyor belt in the first place. And, just possibly, this simpleton had lost count and decided that each box was full enough, hence the missing knives. Anyway, I figured that this wasn't a healthy line of reasoning, so I decided to go with the previously purchased theory (which, I might add, did not make me any less annoyed at the whole situation).

As I approached the counter, the clerk who had processed my order that morning noticed me. I guess she ascertained by the look on my face that I was not happy about having to reappear in their store. As I walked up she put on her best game face and politely asked, "Can I help you?" I sat the bag on the counter, grasped the bottom of the bag, and jerked my hand upwards. When I did, the cutlery flew everywhere. As the contents of the bag dropped onto the counter, the room filled with the sound of metal clanging against metal. The utensils bounced all over the counter, and a few pieces loudly struck the floor. Several people stood behind me waiting for their order to come off the conveyor belt. They slowly backed away from the commotion, which amused me in my mildly deranged state; I knew that they would probably be interested in what I had to say, especially if they were purchasing any kind of silverware. The clerk stood gingerly back from the counter and asked me the obvious. "I'm sorry," she simpered, "Is there a problem?" I snatched the box off the counter and pointed to the front label, which said *place setting for four*, and I asked her, rather aggressively, "What does this say?" She meekly replied, "Place setting for four." I grabbed the only knife that was in the pack, held it up and said, "Then, can you explain to me why there is only one knife in this set?" She apologized and asked me if I would like to exchange it for a new set. I barked, "Yes, *of course I would.* I have dinner guests coming to my house in less than five hours, and I think it would be nice if they could all have a knife with which to butter their bread!"

She nervously collected utensils off the counter and even grabbed the two that fell onto the floor. She kept me in her sight the whole time. I don't think she trusted me, even with just a butter knife, in my current frame of mind; I don't think I blame her. She quickly positioned herself in front of the computer and started the transaction to replace my defective order. I couldn't see what she was typing, but I noticed that she became more and more uneasy as she proceeded. I presumed her nervousness resulted from her dealings with an irate customer. *Little did I know just how big that snowball was going to get that day.* She sheepishly turned around to face me and said, "Uh, well . . . we are out of stock on that item."

Speechless, I stood there, not making a move. I knew that my brain was close to burning out a circuit imperative to its operation. I also knew that if I opened my mouth, I could not control the words that would spring freely from the frustration and anger building in my febrile brain. She quickly reminded me that there were two other stores in the metropolitan area that may have complete sets of the flatware I so desperately longed for. I said, "*Great.* Now, why don't you get on the damn phone and find out so that I don't have to drive all over town to fix your screw up!"

She didn't even reply but instead quickly ran over to the phone and dialed a number. I couldn't hear her conversation, but I could tell she had one wish at that moment: to get me the hell out of her store. She had her back to me, which I thought was rather brave, but she kept intermittently glancing over her shoulder. I really expected the SWAT team to rush in at any time, but after a few minutes, she hung up and told me that their eastside store had a set and they were holding it for me. She said she could refund my money and then I could go to the other store and purchase the other set, but I wasn't about to relinquish the set I had. I thought, if worse came to worse, I could at a minimum use the forks and spoons.

The clock quickly approached 2:00 in the afternoon and I kicked into overdrive. I jumped in the car and hit the road in no time flat. The dilemma of getting to the eastside store was that no freeways ran in that direction; the only way to get there was following the dreaded surface streets the whole way. *Rolling, rolling, snowball's getting bigger.* I estimated that it would take me at least fifteen minutes to get there, *if* I hit every light when it glowed green. I drove as fast as I could, knowing that the way my day had started, I was destined to get a speeding ticket if I drove one mile over the speed limit. With extraordinary effort, I maintained what composure I had left and arrived at the store in decent time.

I jumped out of the car and sprinted into the store as if my life depended upon it. I gripped the bag firmly, and as I ran, the flatware rattled, just as if I were Santa pulling his sleigh, with its jingling bells, spoons and forks. Apparently, the clerk at the other store had alerted the eastside staff as to what I looked like, since they seemed to warily anticipate my arrival. Of course, she might have simply told them to keep an eye out for a crazy woman who looked like she had just been dragged behind a truck for the entire morning. When I walked up, they said, "Mrs. St. George?" I was a little surprised, but pleased that I didn't have to go through any in-depth explanations. My wits were completely spent by that time, and I just said, "Yeah, just empty the box on the counter because I want to count every piece before I take it home with me." The clerk pulled out the box and we proceeded verifying that it truly contained a place setting for four.

Everything seemed to be in order, at last, so I handed over the defective set in exchange for the complete set. I disappeared out the door in a heartbeat. As I ran to the car, I peeked at my watch. I thought, "Okay, I can make it home comfortably before 3:00. That gives me three hours to shower and cook. I'll be fine." Even though I had long since surrendered my dream of relaxing before my guests arrived that evening, I kept focused by repeating the last, comforting phrase in my mind. *I'll be fine.*

I jumped in the car, started it up, and pulled out of the parking lot while I mentally reviewed all the courses that I had planned for dinner. I tried to evaluate the best order in which to prepare everything, so that I could develop the most time-efficient plan. I knew I didn't have any time to spare, since three hours did not allow room for error. I sat at a red light, feeling frazzled, and I could feel my hands trembling as I grasped the wheel. I was glad that I didn't shower that morning because I knew that a hot shower would refresh me, and I prayed that it would rejuvenate my energy as well. When the light finally turned green and I pushed on the accelerator—on the home stretch—the car lunged forward and then promptly died. A totally disoriented feeling rushed over me. A few seconds before, I was deep in thought, trying to salvage the rest of my day. Suddenly, alarmed consciousness filled my mind as the car sat there in the middle of the intersection, not responding to any of my commands. *That damned snowball was now enormous and flying down the mountain out of control!*

I put the car in neutral and spoke to God for a moment. I pleaded that, if I had ever done anything good in my life, I needed his help that afternoon. I closed my eyes, took a deep, cleansing breath, and when I turned the key, the engine started. Cautious relief spread through me as I placed the gearshift in the drive position and pushed on the accelerator. The car lunged forward and then lost power; I turned the key, started the engine again, and lurched forward an inch or two, before losing power. Gritting my teeth, I went through the same motions. Repeat. Stop. Repeat. Stop. I chugged into the first service station I came across and found a non-conspicuous spot to park.

As I turned off the ignition, I sat back and thought I should take a minute just to breathe. *In with the good air, out with the bad* air. No words could describe my feelings at that moment. It ranged somewhere between the feeling of defeat and the feeling of abject despair. I felt like a totally pathetic, unwashed woman with no transportation and a set of utensils by my side. As I sat there wondering what disaster would befall me next, I knew that some things were just not meant to be. There are some things you can control, and some things you can't. *A snowball rolling down a steep hill sometimes cannot be stopped.* I sat there for a few minutes, shaking my head in disbelief. My body trembled, as my eyes started to well up with tears of frustration. Then, I got angry. I jumped out of the car and screamed, shaking my fist against the sky, "I HATE FRIGGING SNOW!" A gentleman who serviced his car at one of the nearby gas pumps quickly returned the fuel nozzle to its resting place, all the time ensuring that he didn't turn his back on me for more than a second. He then hopped into his car and quickly left. I knew he thought I was a complete lunatic—after all, it was the middle of June.

I climbed back in the car and sat there for about five minutes reflecting on my predicament. I concluded that these five minutes would have to suffice for the relaxation time that I had so perfectly planned into that day's schedule. I knew the time had come for me to spring back into action. I reached for my cell phone and called Robert. I told him I didn't care what he was doing at that moment, nothing could measure up in importance to the fact that he needed to drive into town and rescue me, and he needed to do it like a superhero. My location was approximately a twenty-five to thirty minute drive from the house, so I generously gave him twenty minutes to get there. After all, his driving record lay at stake, not mine. And his record was far from perfect already, I might add. Even though I took every opportunity to remind him of that, I knew that if he got a ticket that day, it would be on me. I figured that, if he did get a ticket hurrying to pick me up that afternoon, this would just be the icing on the shit cake that I was being forced to eat that day. It didn't really matter, though, because I knew the way my day was going, his car would probably break down on his way to rescue me. This vision of Steve and Janice arriving at the house, knocking on the door, and wondering why no one was there to greet them kept recurring in my head.

I believe my conversation with God helped, because Robert arrived about twenty-five minutes later. He thought the best option would be to attempt to drive the car to the dealership. He suggested that I follow him in his car. Astonishingly enough, we arrived at the dealership, although every time he stopped for a light, for a car turning in front of him, or just for the hell of it, the car's engine died. But he just started it up again and kept going. No matter what else you might be able to say about Robert, one thing is for certain: the man is persistent.

When we pulled into the dealership, I jumped out, ran inside and explained the problem. I told them that I would just leave the vehicle and pick it up the following week. As we walked back to get into Robert's car, he diplomatically took the car keys from me and said that he thought he should drive. I couldn't disagree with him, since I knew I was in no condition to operate heavy machinery. I did, however, still have enough wits about me that I grabbed the bag containing the newly purchased flatware out of my disabled car, and we continued on our way back home.

When Steve and Janice arrived at the house, precisely at 6:00 p.m., my hair was still wet from my shower as I frantically chopped vegetables for the salad. After quick introductions, Janice handed me a magnum of Chardonnay. It was at that point that I realized that she was clearly an angel sent straight from heaven. I immediately calmed down, took a big gulp of wine, and started to relax.

Even though all of my plans for the perfect evening had collapsed into thin air, as it turned out, we had a wonderful evening. Dinner tasted terrific, although we didn't eat until after eight. They didn't seem to mind, since the magnum of wine that they had brought had been totally consumed by that time, along with both of the bottles that I had purchased. I knew that there was just one thing left to do at that point: swallow my wine snobbery and break out the five-liter cardboard box of wine in the refrigerator. That sustained us through the rest of the evening.

They enjoyed the story of the elusive flatware, which I divulged to them over dinner. Ironically, Janice told me that she was quite nervous about meeting me and worried incessantly about making a good impression. Of course by that time, we were all tanked and nobody cared any more about impressing anybody. In the end, *that snowball of chaos* didn't matter because it was the new friendship I made that evening that made the day special, despite all the frustration that it took to get to that point.

I do want to add that I still use that same flatware nearly every day. Although I've owned it for many years now, it still looks as good as the day I bought it. Not that it really matters, though, because I've already decided that I'll use plastic utensils before I make another attempt at purchasing another place setting for four. After all, plastic ware can be purchased in packages of a hundred and I would never know if a few pieces were missing.

There's More Than One Shade of Black

Driving your vehicle on a really dark evening, when no stars or moon shine in the sky can be challenging at best. When it is pitch dark outside, with full cloud cover overhead, it doesn't matter how bright your headlights radiate; especially if the road is wet and the moon hovers far above a blanket of clouds, the beams from your headlights become absorbed by the black asphalt beneath your vehicle. It's like a black hole, a bottomless abyss that sucks every speck of illumination into its depths. You're blind to details. These exact conditions existed one evening when Tara ventured out for a night of fun with a new group of friends.

One day at work, Tara got a call from one her friends, Anna, who said that their group needed a substitute mahjong player. Anna told Tara via voicemail to call her as soon as possible because, if Tara couldn't participate, they wouldn't have enough players and they would have to cancel the game. The complication of Tara not knowing the rules of Mahjong didn't concern Anna; she simply thought Tara would enjoy a girl's night out. When Tara called her back, Anna said that it didn't matter that Tara didn't know how to play, because they could teach her as they went along. Anna described it as a fairly simple game. She said all the women just show up, bring food, and enjoy each other's company. Tara decided that she wanted to give it a try and told Anna that she would happily join them. Tara enjoys meeting new people anyway—and you already know the thing about her (and me) being born with a deck of cards in our hands. It seemed like the perfect opportunity to have a fun evening and put her talents to good use.

It just so happened that a woman named Ann (not to be confused with the aforementioned Ann*a*) hosted the game that evening.

Apparently, Ann (the one without the extra "a") had inherited her home from her relatives and it was supposedly something special. Anna told Tara that, even if she wasn't that interested in playing Mahjong, it would be worth her time just to witness Ann's residence. Ann's husband had evidently passed away a few years ago and the house had been in the family for many years. According to Anna, it was *to die for*. This cinched the deal for Tara; she would definitely participate.

When you live out in the country, as does Tara, you don't get directions like "just go to 4th and Main, hang a right and we'll be the third house on your left." When you live in a rural area, directions consist of notable landmarks. Living in a rural area myself, I have often wondered why this is so, and I have reached the conclusion that it has to be one of two reasons. One, since there are very few street markers deep in the rural areas of the country, it would make no sense to tell someone to turn onto a road with a name that is not clearly identified anywhere. The conversation would go something like, "Take the highway to Old Miner's Road and hang a right." "Where is Old Miner's Road?" "It's the one past the second cow pasture after the S-curve following the cemetery." Telling someone the name of an unidentified road is simply a waste of breath. Two, I believe that the only people who know the true names of the unidentified thoroughfares have been long dead, and so the names of many of these anonymous roads have been lost for generations.

The directions that Tara received that night resembled the description above. Anna told Tara to go down Highway 33 to Bethany Church Road. At that point, Anna told Tara to drive past Bethany Church and then continue driving by a structure that used to be a school, but wasn't anymore. When Tara spotted two white pillars on each side of a driveway, she would be at Ann's house. Anna explained to Tara that Ann's house wasn't visible from the road, but if she turned onto the driveway with the white pillars, it would lead her to the house. After receiving these directions, Tara realized that Ann only lived about ten minutes from her house. Still, she thought she should play it safe and allow herself about twenty minutes to get there, just in case she made a wrong turn. After all, as the new player in the group, she didn't want to delay the game by being late.

The thick layer of clouds overhead had just started to spit snow when Tara left her house for Ann's. The roads glistened with moisture as the flakes melted immediately after making contact with the warm surface. In addition, the pitch black sky made it difficult for Tara to distinguish where the edges of the road ended. The headlights didn't reflect any light off the pavement; it was as if the black road absorbed every lumen emanating from Tara's headlights. She had a difficult time seeing anything. Her windshield began to fog up, so Tara attempted to clear it with her hand, but her actions only managed to smear the moisture that had accumulated on the window. The mess created by her efforts made it even more difficult to discriminate subtle details along the roadside. Fortunately, Tara had lived in the area for almost ten years by then, so she knew the back roads fairly well. She managed to find the right road and, after passing what she thought must have been the old school, she happened upon the two white pillars on either side of Ann's driveway, and slowly turned in.

The first thing that struck Tara about Ann's driveway was that it appeared immaculate. Tara is accustomed to long driveways, because hers encompasses about three-tenths of a mile long. But it was winter and Tara's driveway—and, for that matter every other gravel driveway that she had recently driven on—remained filled with potholes and washed out areas. Practically everyone that lives in the area has either dirt or gravel driveways, as it is just too difficult to maintain cement or asphalt roads, not to mention too expensive to pay for the upkeep. But although the night appeared extremely dark and specific features hid obscurely, Ann's driveway seemed as smooth as silk. Tara couldn't differentiate the exact material of which the driveway was constructed, but the ride felt smooth and uninterrupted, as if no flaws existed on the perfect surface. Although she couldn't see clearly, the driveway appeared paved, because the color looked uniformly dark and evenly distributed. Tara thought, "Holy Cow, this woman must be loaded," (and she was not referring to a drug habit).

Tara continued up the driveway until she spotted the house. The old, southern-style mansion stood in the distance like a welcome beacon in the dark night. Although the porch light beamed, it still didn't offer much additional light on such a moonless evening. Tara decided that, before she parked, she should confirm that she had located the right house. Then she could ask Ann where she should park her truck. She pulled up the circular drive, until she sat right in front of the door. The front door stood open, but the storm door remained closed. An adolescent girl in a pink robe stood inside the house peering out. Tara rolled down her window expecting that the girl would open the door so Tara could ask her if she was in the right place. But the girl just stood there looking at Tara. Tara started thinking that she would be forced to have to get out of the truck and go up to the front door, when a lady appeared at the door and opened it. The lady leaned out and said, "Can I help you?" Tara said, "I'm looking for Ann Miller." The woman replied, "That is I." Tara thought, "Ooh, that sounded a little formal," but Tara knew that this woman came from money, so she expected that Ann might have a composed, slightly distant type of demeanor. Tara leaned out the truck window with a smile on her face and cheerfully said, "Oh great. Hi. I'm Tara. I'm here to play Mahjong with the group tonight. Just tell me where you would like me to leave my truck." The woman coldly replied, "Yes, this *is* where we are playing Mahjong tonight but I would appreciate it if you would start by backing your truck off of my lawn! Go over there behind those bushes and leave your vehicle in the parking area!"

Tara felt totally embarrassed and started rambling aimlessly. She said, "I am so sorry. I thought this was a circular drive. It's so dark out I couldn't really see and it's also very wet." At that point Tara thought it was just best to start driving. On her way over to the parking area, Tara decided to try and find a big rock to crawl under, but as I mentioned, the lawn was so immaculate, not one rock emerged in sight. She did manage to find the parking area and parked her truck in a more appropriate spot than she previously drove into.

After parking, she sat there in her truck praying that one of the other women would show up before she had to go in the house. After making a complete fool out of herself, she didn't want to face her new acquaintance alone. Obviously, Tara thought Ann must already hate her, and the thought of making conversation alone with her terrified Tara. Of course, Tara had left a few minutes early just in case she got lost, and as luck would have it, all the other women, it seemed, ran late. Tara didn't want to be too obvious about delaying her entrance until the others arrived, so after a few minutes Tara bravely got out of her truck and walked towards the house.

When Tara climbed the stairs to the house, Ann received her politely if a little coldly. Ann gave Tara a booklet that explained the rules of the game and Tara sat in a stiff chair and studied it, continuing to pass the awkward time. Once the others arrived, they proceeded to teach Tara how to play. Preparing for the festivities, the women unpacked the snacks and stuff that they had brought for the evening. Tara had brought a bottle of wine, so she pulled it out of a brown paper bag and said to the others, "Thanks for inviting me. I brought some wine for everyone." Ann politely said to Tara, "Oh, lovely. Let me get you a corkscrew," as she rose gracefully from her chair and headed towards the kitchen. Tara turned to her and said, "Oh, that's okay. It's a twist-off." Obviously, Tara really impressed the hell out of Ann that night. First, she barreled up to the front door in her 4x4 truck, doing who knows how much damage to this woman's immaculately cared-for lawn, and then she'd brought wine that would never have even a passing acquaintance with the concept of "aging."

Tara wondered if she would ever make it through that night, but in the end, she felt that Ann actually took a liking to her. I think it probably had something to do with sympathy for the "less fortunate" (or "less sane") people of the world. Once Tara left that night she felt certain that she would never be invited back, but she also knew she did the best she could, given the circumstances.

The middle of the following week, Anna called Tara and said they needed another fill-in for Mahjong that week. Tara couldn't believe it, but thought that she had to redeem herself and go. And guess where they played? Yes, it just so happened that Ann was hosting the evening again. Tara wanted so desperately to be given another chance, so she thought that it would be best to just laugh at the whole situation and move on. She seriously hoped that Ann felt as congenial.

When Tara entered Ann's house for the second time, she walked straight up to her and said, "I saw that my parking spot was open, so I just pulled up right to the front door!" All the women got a good laugh out of that and from then on, Tara became a regular member of the women's Mahjong club. I might note that whenever the girls have a new member join the club, especially if the first meeting starts a bit awkward, they always share the story of Tara's first encounter with Ann and her home. The tale always breaks the tension and offers the audience a good, healthy laugh. I have to agree that Tara's first attendance at the Mahjong club was truly one of Tara's classic moments. In her attempt to be friendly and polite, she ended up stepping in quicksand. She just made sure from that point on that, when she went to play Mahjong with the women, she wore her waders.

Sometimes Shit Happens

One of the most fulfilling experiences that I have had in my sixty-plus years of existence is that of being a grandmother. I thought I loved my children more than I could love anything or anyone else, but I was wrong. My grandchildren are my most cherished treasures.

The saga began with a precious girl born in January of 2000. The idea of being a grandmother thrilled me, even though the kids hadn't bothered getting married prior to bearing offspring. I didn't feel the urge to climb up on my soapbox regarding that subject. I had just recently gotten divorced and as such, I wasn't a big fan of marriage at the time. When I had children, I did not get blessed with a girl. Not that I cared either way, but the chance of helping to raise a young lady excited me. Although, I became concerned when my son Eric told me they decided to name her Tyranny.

Despite her name, the first few years of her life occurred uneventfully. She always had a purpose for her tears. When she cried we would discover that she was hungry or wet. Either way, once the situation became remedied, she relapsed back into the happy child we had always known. When she started walking, she reacted to disciplinary comments, such as "no" and "don't touch that" calmly and obediently. We cohabited effortlessly with her just as I had imagined my life as a grandmother would be.

When Tyranny turned three years old, we learned that she had a sibling on the way. As my enjoyment of her knew no bounds, the news thrilled me beyond belief. I couldn't wait for the arrival of grandchild number two. In April of 2003, my grandson entered the world. Eric and Nikki named him Draven. Even though the name was uncommon, I liked it. It didn't have a negative connotation to it like his sister's moniker. Little did I know that maybe it should have since over time he would earn such a name, over and over again.

Draven did not grow into a toddler gracefully like his sister. His constant demands frustrated me. His disposition ranged from fastidious to extreme agitation, no matter what day or circumstance. Tyranny understood what the phrase *inside voice* meant. Draven defied the rules and shrieked repeatedly when he disagreed with the situation. There is no doubt in my mind that his squeal could shatter glass. The shrillness of his siren boomed in an octave higher than any human being's audio sense should register. Needless to say, I always had a good supply of earplugs on hand.

When he became mobile, I knew the torture had just begun. His curiosity knew no boundaries. He disturbed everything within his reach. We couldn't leave anything lying around because he had a fascination with making inanimate objects airborne. If it had buttons on it, such as the remote control, he pushed them. If it had doors on it, he opened them just to slam them shut. I often wondered if he had hearing damage, since abrupt, deafening sounds filled his world. If he doesn't, he certainly will have because the human eardrum can only withstand a certain decibel level for long periods of time without sustaining some kind of permanent hearing loss. One day I inserted earplugs into his ears, hoping to lessen the effect of his self-inflicted, stentorian surroundings, only to discover that the act increased the intensity of his destructive behavior.

When Draven approached his second birthday, he learned a new trick that surpassed all the others in his short history, although the list is long and distinguished. He became fascinated with his own bowel movements. He loved to stick his hand down into his diaper for prolonged periods of time. Although I didn't experience that challenge with my two boys, many of my girlfriends who have sons told me that their boys continually stuck their hands down their pants, fascinated by what lie beneath. I discerned this trait early on with

Draven and even though I tried to discourage that particular behavior, his determination to do things I disapproved of outlasted my will to make him cease and desist.

One weekend I watched Tyranny and Draven while Eric and Nikki worked. The morning had come and gone and the hands on the clock approached naptime for Draven (which I might add had become my favorite time of the day). When he was younger, I put him in a crib at naptime, with the television tuned into the cartoon network. He would quietly watch cartoons until he fell asleep. But as he got older, Draven started crawling out of his crib like a jungle monkey, although his stature is vertically challenged. Most of his shortness is in his legs, so I would have thought it humanly impossible for him to crawl out of his crib without breaking his neck. But the little scoundrel did it every time, therefore, so much for the crib as a refuge and so much for an hour of quiet time for Grandma.

That afternoon, I walked into the living room and turned on the cartoon channel. I took Draven's sippy cup and filled it with chocolate milk, hoping that he would lie on the floor quietly, at least long enough for him to slip into slumber. Usually while he is settling into his nap, I have to covertly check up on him because if he sees me, he instantly jumps up and starts screeching (I am beginning to form a comparison with the earlier jungle monkey comment). I quietly walked up to the edge of the doorway and peered around the corner to check on the status of his somnolence. I observed his eyelids, which had grown heavy, although he still maintained a death grip on the sippy cup. I also noticed that the liquid inside the cup had greatly diminished, so I knew it wouldn't be long before the sandman took over his consciousness.

I walked back to the kitchen and continued my pursuit of making the perfect baby back rib. I busily worked assembling the ribs on the rotisserie and making the basting sauce. I think approximately fifteen minutes had passed before Tyranny charged into the room, yelling,

"Grandma! Grandma! Draven did a very bad thing", which I might add is the worst six words in the English language.

Although my forearms were saturated with pork fat and the pork blood extruding from the raw meat, I quickly became concerned for the safety of my grandchild. Not knowing the full meaning of *a very bad thing*, I lifted my forearms towards the ceiling, in order to prevent dripping any of the plasma onto the floor and ran towards the living room. As I reached the halfway point from the kitchen to the living room, I smelled a rancid odor. I immediately knew that Draven had experienced a bowel movement, and due to the intensity of the effluvium emanating from the locality, it smelled like a doozy.

As I rounded the corner leading into the living room, I witnessed the most horrific thing I had ever seen in my entire life. Draven had reached into his diaper, pulled out a turd, and proceeded to smear it all over the coffee table. I appeared he had repeated this action several times, and in addition, he had taken off his tennis shoes and ran them through the mess as well. I thundered, "Draven, what are you doing?" As he innocently looked up at me I noticed the feces covering his cheeks. Although my abrupt presence in the room startled him, he continued his task of smearing the poop in a circular pattern, taking great care to completely cover the entire tabletop, as if he were a brilliant artist inspired by his own work.

The gag reflex kicked in, and I began dry heaving. As I raised my hands up to my mouth, the smell of the pork blood induced an equal reaction to the initial gagging. I ran back into the kitchen and turned the water on, quickly rinsing my hands and splashing cold water on my face to calm my senses. I took a paper towel and after drying my arms and hands, I pressed it against my forehead. I knew I had to re-enter the war zone and attempt to cleanse the evil sprite that I knew as my grandson. I also knew it wouldn't happen without a lot of discomfort on my part.

As I apprehensively strolled down the hallway to the living room, I covered my nose and mouth with the damp paper towel. I thought that might possibly reduce the effects of the fumes and aid in my swiftness to clean up the child and his artwork. I stood in the doorway, watching as Draven began his pursuit of covering yet another surface with his excrement. I walked up behind him, grabbed him with my free hand, pulled him close to my hip and proceeded to sprint upstairs to the bathroom. I put him in the tub, diaper and all. I carefully unsecured the tape, trying to avoid contact with his feces that now covered about fifty percent of his body. Once I had removed the diaper, I turned on the water and proceeded to wash him with a wet cloth. Once the visible crap had disappeared, I filled up the tub with warm water, dumping a quart of soap into the water.

One thing that I didn't notice when I first started the scouring process was the condition of his fingernails. Dark-colored poop caked the crease under each nail and he continually touched his face with them and ran them through his hair. I eventually took a nailbrush and scrubbed each finger one at a time, fighting the bedeviled imp the whole time. Finally, he smelled human once more. I breathed a sigh of relief, although I knew I still had to tackle the mess he created in the living room.

I marched downstairs with Draven on my hip and placed him on the couch. After my lecture of something resembling, "If you get off that couch before I clean up this crap, you will wish you hadn't". I mean, come on. If shitting all over yourself and smearing your feces all over the living room doesn't get you killed, just how frightened do you think he was about getting off that couch? As I contemplated that very issue while walking to the kitchen to fetch every clean supply know to women, the hint of a smile appeared on my face. That's when I knew I had been inducted into the Grandmothers' Club. Anyone that can smile while only halfway through the worse mess they had ever encountered must be completely insane, or totally blinded by love. I guess I'm guilty as charged (on both counts).

I took the bucket, half full of warm water and a generous portion of Mr. Clean, into the living room and proceeded to wipe off every flat surface in my living room. The coffee table and other flat surfaces weren't difficult to clean. I threw the shoes outside, which I thought would serve as a suitable job for my son when he arrived to pick up Satan's spawn. The next problem I encountered revealed itself when I focused my attention on the decorative carving, delicately etched on all four sides of the coffee table. The little bastard ensured that he packed every crevice with crap, which had dried into a cement-like substance. I worked on the engraving for an hour, just me and a toothpick (now there's an afternoon of fun). Here's a hint for all of you prospective grandparents out there. Don't buy furniture with delicate carvings or that has any surface that is not completely flat and smooth. If the furniture has any kind of indentation, don't take it to your house. If you currently own furniture like that, sell it. Save yourself from the torture that your grandchildren will put you through and the hours of agony keeping it clean.

Being a member of the Grandmothers' Club has given me a different perspective on life. Every time a younger person casually comments about shit happening, I think to myself that they have no idea what that phrase means. I, however, have experienced shit happening first hand. Regardless, my adoration for my grandson continues, despite his devious nature. Although Draven has tested my patience, and frankly my sanity, in his short life on this earth, I wouldn't give him up, not for a hundred just like him. (Oh, I shudder at the very thought!)

Warming Up to Things

As I get older, I find every day seems to offer up a new challenge. Although I'm void of the struggles of my younger years, such as raising children while holding a full-time job, I am continually confronted with new tests of my fortitude. These trials, while seemingly less life-changing, still present turmoil in my daily routine. I tell myself that I've earned the right to miss deadlines, procrastinate, and even completely forget things as times since I am well past my fifth decade on this earth, although it doesn't make it less frustrating when I do.

When my father passed middle age, he informed me that he had developed a condition called CRS. When I asked him what CRS was, he replied, "Can't Remember Shit." I chuckled, assuming that he was joking. As I age, I realize his condition was not a joke at all, as I have the same condition now. For example, the other day, while picking up around the house, I remembered that I needed to take out some hamburger meat for dinner that evening. The grandkids had decided to spend the weekend with me and I told them I would make them cheeseburgers for dinner. I headed towards the utility room, where my full-size freezer resides. When I passed the bathroom on my way, I noticed that the rug lay crumpled up in the corner (dang those cats). So I flipped on the light and went into the bathroom, tidying up the rug. I also noticed that the sink needed to be cleaned, so I reached into the cabinet for the Scrubbing Bubbles and proceeded to make the basin and faucet spotless.

Leaving the bathroom I continued in my efforts of tidying up, since the grandkids were due to arrive in the next few hours. Going about my routine, I again remembered that I needed to take the hamburger out of the freezer. I headed that way, repeating in my mind, *get out the burger; get out the burger,* as I walked down the hall towards the utility room. When I opened the freezer door, a small block of ice hit the floor. I noticed that a significant amount of ice and frost had formed on the inside top of the freezer. This phenomenon had occurred before, several times. My freezer is over thirty years old, and the hinges on the door tend to loosen up with use, which causes a break in the seal and the freezer frosts up excessively along the front, top edge. When I start getting too much frost on the top, I'm required to tighten up the hinges to remedy the situation. I headed to the garage, got the socket set, and tightened up the door. I tested it a few times, checking the seals to make sure the door set squarely against the frame. Everything seemed to be in order, so I returned the tools to the garage and continued my quest of making sure the house was clean in time for Tyranny and Draven's arrival.

I decided to run the dishwasher, since I wanted it to be empty for their visit. The grandkids tend to dirty a lot of dishes, since they frequent the kitchen for various drinks and snacks outside of the normal meal times. I opened the dishwasher door, added the liquid detergent, and after closing the door, set the dishwasher to the heavy setting and turned it on. Remembering once again about the hamburger meat, I knew by that time I would probably have to partially defrost it in the microwave by that time, which I hated to do because the edges sometimes get browned in the process, leaving bits of cooked meat in the raw burger, making it cook less evenly. Regardless, I knew they loved their burgers, so I headed for the third time towards the laundry room, just when my cat Charlie decided to lose his lunch all over my freshly mopped floor. He wretched, walked a few steps and vomited again, giving me a quick glance before heading out of the hallway. "Oh, Charlie," I pleaded, wanting to wring his neck but instead, I grabbed the paper towels. I wiped up the mess and grabbed a clean rag, wetting it and polishing up the tile to its previous state.

An hour later when the grandkids came bounding through the front door, I had completed my housekeeping duties. I am always happy to see them and vice versa (at least they appear so). We hugged as they off-loaded their backpacks in the entry way and I exchanged hellos and good-byes with their mother Nikki. After she left, of course the kids were hungry. They asked, "Grandma, can we have our burgers now? We're starving." My heart sank as I knew I had never completed the task of removing the burger from the freezer. My CRS had control that day, which reduced my attention span to that of a two-year-old child. Shaking my head in disgust, I replied, "How about pizza instead?" After all, by now I have the local pizzeria on speed dial, and they even deliver. It's a good thing too because I'm fairly certain after a few times of me forgetting to pick up my order they would refuse to do business with me.

Tara suffers from CRS as well and the results are the same as they continue to complicate her life, as well as her husband's Pete's. One day recently, after hours of completing tasks on Tara's honey-to-do list on the farm, Pete retired to the house, desperately seeking a hot shower. A few of Tara's friends had stopped by, so she chatted aimlessly with them while Pete returned to the house. Dusk had come and gone by that time and the pastures had turned dark, so Tara and her friends hung out in the lighted stables. One little tidbit of knowledge about Tara's and Pete's farm is that they get water from a well. The well fully sustains the household and water for the animals, that is, unless they use too much, or if someone leaves the water running outside, which drains the well.

As Tara chatted endlessly with her guests, she heard a sharp voice. Pete bellowed out of the bedroom window, "Tara! Did you leave the water on?" Immediately, Tara thought, *Oh Shit!* But knowing that after toiling in the fields all day, taking care of all of her animal's needs, all Pete wanted at that time and moment was a warm shower, she yelled, "I don't' know. Let me check!" She knew Pete felt irritated, just as much as she knew she'd left the water on. But in her effort to avoid confrontation and since the sun had set an hour earlier, she crept out across the pasture to the water spout and turned it off. She crept back to the barn and walked to the front, yelling, "I don't see any water on! Just give it a minute and try again!"

Another day, soon after, Tara was helping Pete complete chores around the farm. She really doesn't help, but stands by in case he needs something, since she wants to support him, especially since he's doing work for her horse farm. Pete's task that day consisted of fixing a gate on one of the pastures. Pete asked Tara to run to the shed and get him a Phillips-head screwdriver. She nodded and obediently headed towards the shed. On her way, she noticed a hose strung across the yard that she had left out the night before when she filled the troughs up with water. She grabbed the end, coiling it up as she walked along, and returned it to its proper place alongside of the barn. As she laid it down, she saw a pitchfork that she uses to gather hay laying on the ground. She thought, *I'll need that later*, so she picked it up and carried it over to the hay shed. When she arrived, a wheelbarrow sat beside the shed, which needed to be dumped, so she rolled it over to the edge of the pasture and dumped the contents, then returned the wheelbarrow beside the shed. She then grabbed the broom and started sweeping the shed out. In the distance, she heard Pete shout, "Tara! What are you doing?" Tara yelled back, "I'm sweeping! Why?" Highly frustrated, Pete shouted, "Where's the hell's the screwdriver that I need!" Of course, Tara had forgotten all about her original task of retrieving the screwdriver for Pete. But as she became quickly reminded, she yelled, "Coming", as she sprinted into the shed, grabbed the screwdriver, and raced across the pasture towards Pete. Thank goodness she hasn't forgotten how to run!

Speaking of CRS, not only has it caused me to disappoint my grandchildren, it has presented even greater challenges in my life. When I was in my early forties, my gynecologist informed me that I needed a hysterectomy. Given the option of keeping my ovaries or having them removed, I told my doctor to take out anything and everything he could get to that I no longer needed. I said, "Doc, if you have to go in there, make it worth your time and mine." I had my appendix removed when I was young, but still having my gall bladder and knowing many friends who have had theirs removed after complications, I asked him to take that as well, hopefully sparing me another surgery later. He refused to go that far but did perform a complete hysterectomy, which required me to take hormone replacements.

A year ago after my annual visit, my doctor told me that I should wean myself off my estrogen pills. He said that I was past the age of menopause, so although I no longer needed the medication, I couldn't just quit taking it cold turkey. After asking him why, his reply was something along the lines of having the hot flash from hell. That got my attention, so we discussed the proper procedure of removing the estrogen from my daily routine. His suggestion was for me to first reduce the pills by one pill per week, taking six instead of seven each week, and stick with that for three to four weeks. He said if I didn't show any signs of hot flashes, then reduce my intake to five pills per week for three to four weeks, and so on until the time that I weaned myself completely off the replacement therapy.

I hate taking pills in the morning so I looked forward to reducing my morning dosage by removing the estrogen from my routine. I decided that initially I would not take the pill on Sundays. Monday through Saturday I swallowed an estrogen pill and skipped the dose on Sundays. I continued with this behavior for four weeks, just to be safe. Then I began to skip my morning dose on Wednesdays as well. After the next four weeks passed and experiencing no signs of hot flashes, I decided to reduce my intake by another pill.

I definitely overanalyzed the situation. While determining whether I should take four weekly pills, each on Monday, Tuesday,

Thursday, and Saturday or on Monday, Wednesday, Friday, and Saturday, I became frustrated. I decided the best course of action would be just to take a pill every other day. So when Monday morning came, I took a pill, as well as Wednesday, Friday, and the following Sunday. The second week I knew I had to take my pill Tuesday, Thursday, and Saturday. Everything was going well, still with no signs of hot flashes, until week three or four. After repeating the every-other-day routine for several weeks, I couldn't remember if I had taken a pill the day before or not. And since I didn't mark it down on the calendar when I started, I couldn't look back to determine when the appropriate day to take it was. The following few weeks I just took the pill some mornings and skipped it others, hoping that I was getting the proper dose. Then it occurred to me that I may be increasing my dose, since I could never remember if I took the pill the morning before or not. I became extremely angry at myself and decided to take the plunge, so I tossed the medication in the garbage. I knew that I had weaned myself halfway off the medication by that point, so I figured, *how bad could it really get* even if I experienced hot flashes. At least my timing was good, as the fall had come and gone and we had arrived at the beginning of the winter months.

The first hot flash that I experienced was at work while I was talking to a colleague a few weeks later. I felt my face get hot, but that was the only symptom that I had. She said, "Your face is really red." I told her that I had quit taking my hormone replacements and I guess that's what a hot flash felt like. I didn't think it felt that uncomfortable and was glad that I had weaned myself off the medication instead of just stopping cold turkey. I knew the hot flashes would eventually run their course and I would be back to normal. For the next week or so, I experienced the hot, red face flash once in a while, say every other day. I became fascinated by the rush of heat, and thought it was odd that I only experienced the heat in my face. Regardless, I knew I would have to endure the somewhat uncomfortable symptom for some time to come. The question in my mind was how long I would have to endure the episodes, even if they didn't feel that unnerving.

A month or so after I had tossed my lifeline to normalcy in the garbage, as I sat in my office at work, a surge of heat ran through my body. I thought, "Wow, that's a little stronger than normal." Immediately I shed my jacket that I usually wear year round to comfort me from the coldness of the winter and the cool air conditioning in the summer. Within seconds my face broke out into a sweat. I grabbed a note pad and started fanning myself. The flash lasted about five minutes and then my body returned to its normal state. I took a tissue and wiped the sweat off my forehead and cheeks, feeling lucky that I don't wear face makeup or I would have looked more disheveled than as if I just had a vigorous workout.

Within days, the hot flashes came more frequently and arrived with more vengeance. Not only did I sweat profusely in my facial region, my armpits, back, and (excuse me for saying so), my ass. Yes, can you believe that? I thought, what the hell, my ass is sweating! I swear to you I looked like I had been working out in the heat for hours, dripping wet from the sweat accompanied by my so-call power surges. If I happened to be in a sitting position during the episode, when I rose from my chair, I would have to pull the seat of my pants away from my rump, as they would be stuck. Then I would spend the next thirty minutes fanning my armpits and ass in an attempt to dry out my clothes.

The ultimate hot flash occurred on my way to work on a cold, February morning. I usually leave for work around 6:30 a.m. and the skies are still dark at that time. I had turned on the heat in the car and shivered from the cold air, which the thermometer in my car read eighteen degrees. As I turned onto the freeway, I felt the warming sensation, starting in my abdomen and quickly climbing up my chest. I flipped off the heater and my face immediately felt hot. I rolled down the window, hoping to avoid breaking a sweat first thing in the morning. I felt the dampness on the back of my neck start to form, so I rolled down the other window. My hair was still damp from my morning shower, and the frigid breeze felt amazing. I realized the faster I drove the cooler the air felt, so I pushed hard on the accelerator, passing the seventy miles per hour mark that was the speed limit at that time. Luckily, I live a ways out of town, so I don't have to share the road with many vehicles until I get closer to the city limits.

The faster I drove, the more amazing I felt. My hair flapped haphazardly as the wind whipped through it. The cold air actually burned slightly, but compared to the sweat and discomfort from the heat, I was in heaven. That is until I looked into my rear view mirror to see the flashing lights behind me. I immediately let off the accelerator and pulled over onto the shoulder, stopping a short distance later. I had no idea how fast I was going, but I knew there was a ticket in my future. I sat there with both windows still down, waiting for the officer to approach the car.

When he walked up to the window, he took a double take when he saw me. He asked, "Ma'am, do you know how fast you were going?" I hung my head and said, "No, I have no idea." He replied, "License and proof of insurance please." I dug in my purse and pulled out my license and insurance card, handing them to him. He walked back to the patrol car and got in. I shook my head in disgust. I had driven for over thirty-five years and never once gotten a ticket. I really believed that I could drive my entire life without getting a citation, but I knew that morning it just wasn't meant to be. I looked at myself in the side mirror and saw my hair was frozen, extending straight back and up slightly from the top of my head. I touched it and it felt like frozen spaghetti that had stuck together in strands on the bottom of the pan when you forget to stir it during cooking. I took my hands and tried to muss up my hair, also attempting to thaw it gradually and not break it off. I thought, no wonder he did a double take. I looked like the bride of Frankenstein, minus the gray stripe.

I looked out of my rear-view mirror and saw him getting out of his patrol car, carrying his ticket booklet. He walked up to my window and said, "Ma'am, have you been drinking?" I looked at him, shocked and replied, "Are you crazy! It's 6:30 in the morning!" His serious facial expression didn't waver when he added, "Can I ask you why you were driving ninety-three miles per hour on a cold, February morning with both windows down?" I couldn't believe it. I said to him, "I was going 93?" His expression still did not change, nor did he confirm the speed. He said, "Ma'am, please answer the question."

I blurted out, "I was having the hot flash from hell and the cold air felt good. The faster I drove, the better it felt. I didn't realize that I had surpassed the speed limit." The stoic expression on his face faltered, and I observed his chest heave upwards, such as when a person attempts to hold something back, like a hiccup or throwing up. I waited for him to respond, feeling completely humiliated and foolish. As I studied his expression, I could see the corners of his mouth twitching, as if to suppress a smile. I thought, "This jerk thinks this is funny!" Then a laugh escaped him. He tried to disguise it as a cough, but it was definitely a laugh. He said, "Sorry Ma'am," as the stoic expression returned to his face. He kept fiddling with my license and registration and I could see his hands shaking slightly. He smiled and quickly shook his head as if to ward off some pest buzzing around his face, regaining his indifference. He repeatedly tapped the head of his pen on the citation pad in his hand and I became extremely irritated. The hot flash had subsided, although I looked like a train wreck, and that asshole felt amused by the whole situation. I said, "Look, just write me the ticket so I can be on my way."

Immediately after the words left my mouth, he lost complete control, busting out laughing so vigorously that he doubled over, like he pulled a muscle in his abdomen. He stood upright and gazed down at me with a pitiful look as his mouth twitched up and down, then again howled with laughter, raising his right hand which still held the pen, extending his index finger as if to motion for me to give him a second. I looked up at him, displaying a *fine, go ahead and laugh* expression, shaking my head from side-to-side, waiting for him to regain his composure. I could see tears running down the sides of his face and I prayed to God they would freeze to his face and cause some kind of permanent damage. He coughed, stood straight up, and attempted to say, "Ma'am, I apologize," but couldn't manage to get the entire phrase out of his mouth before gales of laughter exited his mouth. His uncontrollable hilarity sounded like it emanated deep within his guttural region, as his whole body shook from his merriment. He again raised his right hand, in an apologetic gesture, as tears ran steadily down his cheeks in constant streams.

I felt steam rolling off the top of my head, and this time it was not a hot flash, but instead shear agitation at his enjoyment of my plight. Each time he prepared to steady himself, before he could regain control he would again burst into a fit of laughter. Surrendering to the situation, as he continued his endless mirth, he handed me my license and insurance card, waving his right hand while stumbling to say, "Never mind," but not successfully delivering the message between his irrepressible bursts. He returned to the patrol car, turned off his lights and in my rear-view mirror I could see him slumped over the steering wheel with his body shaking violently as he continued to laugh heartily. Bastard!

I started the car, flipped on my turn signal and after seeing that my path was clear, pulled back onto the freeway. I rolled up the windows and flipped on the heater, knowing that I needed to thaw out my hair before arriving at work. Ten minutes later I pulled into my parking space at work. Checking the mirror, I still looked disheveled, but at least my hair had returned to the hanging position. I grabbed the comb out of my purse and quickly ran through it, not really caring what I looked like, but not wanting to scare anyone (or if I'm completely honest, not wanting to send another human being into endless fits of laughter). I didn't feel as if I could take anymore humiliation that morning.

That event occurred three years ago and I'm still experiencing hot flashes. They have become much milder, with very little sweating and mainly a warm feeling at worst. Of course, when I sense the emanate arrival of the heat, I grab the nearest thing in my reach and start to fan myself until the sensation passes. Tara never experienced hot flashes. Of course, she never had a hysterectomy and went through menopause naturally without any symptoms or complications (that bitch!) Just kidding. We laugh about my intermittent power surges and the events that arise as a result. I can still brag about having a perfect driving record though. Tara insists that if the hot flash didn't occur, the officer wouldn't have lost his composure while hearing my ridiculous story and would have cited me. I remind her that if I didn't have the hot flash, I wouldn't have been driving ninety miles per hour either, so it wouldn't be an issue. Either way, I guess I can say that I'm warming up to my sixties.

The Last Word

I think it's time to end the madness, thus, my storytelling escapade. My hope is that when you encounter challenges throughout your life, just think about someone slipping on a banana peel. I know that people can get seriously injured by falling, but as in the cartoons, when someone slips on a banana peel, they never get physically hurt. Their ego may get bruised and they may become somewhat humiliated, but the outcome is always a chuckle while looking at the results of people's silly behavior. I'm going to wrap this up now. Truth be known, I feel a hot flash coming on. I bought a big box fan at a garage sale the other day. It serves me well. I'm going to go, turn it on full blast, and sit in front of it, naked!

www.ingramcontent.com/pod-product-compliance
Lightning Source LLC
Chambersburg PA
CBHW071738150726
47998CB00005B/1695